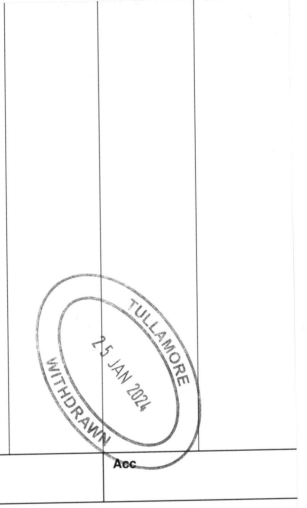

Class	Acc

D1355512

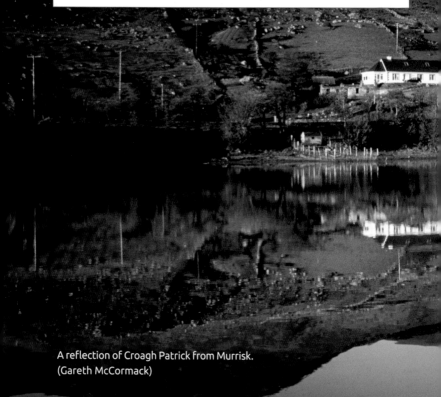

Advice to Readers

Every effort is made by our authors to ensure the accuracy of our guidebooks. However, changes can occur after a book has been printed. If you notice discrepancies between this guidebook and the facts on the ground, please let us know, either by email to enquiries@collinspress.ie or by post to The Collins Press, West Link Park, Doughcloyne, Wilton, Cork, T12 N5EF, Ireland.

A reflection of Croagh Patrick from Murrisk.
(Gareth McCormack)

PILGRIM PATHS IN IRELAND–A GUIDE

FROM SLIEVE MISH TO SKELLIG MICHAEL

John G. O'Dwyer

The Collins Press

Overview Map

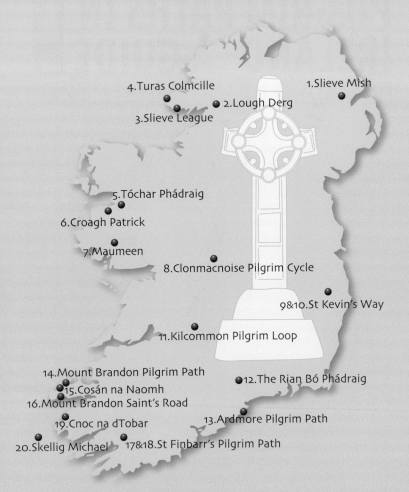

4. Turas Colmcille
1. Slieve Mish
2. Lough Derg
3. Slieve League
5. Tóchar Phádraig
6. Croagh Patrick
7. Maumeen
8. Clonmacnoise Pilgrim Cycle
9&10. St Kevin's Way
11. Kilcommon Pilgrim Loop
14. Mount Brandon Pilgrim Path
15. Cosán na Naomh
16. Mount Brandon Saint's Road
12. The Rian Bó Phádraig
19. Cnoc na dTobar
13. Ardmore Pilgrim Path
20. Skellig Michael
17&18. St Finbarr's Pilgrim Path

Irish Pilgrim Passport

The five pilgrim routes that must be completed in order to obtain a *Teastas* (completion certificate for the Irish Pilgrim Journey) are indicated on the facing page with the symbol: ❁

The routes are the Tóchar Phádraig (route 5 in this book), St Kevin's Way (routes 9 and 10), Cosán na Naomh (route 15), St Finbarr's Pilgrim Path (routes 17 and 18) and Cnoc na dTobar (route 19). Fully stamped passports are then forwarded to Ballintubber Abbey, Claremorris, County Mayo to obtain the *Teastas*.

Information correct at time of writing. See www.pilgrimpath.ie for more details.

Contents

Waymarking post for Lough Derg Pilgrim Path, County Donegal. (Gareth McCormack)

Introduction

Often I have wondered why it is that rooted within almost every belief system is an ageless tradition of a penitential journey to a place that has been elevated to a higher spiritual plane. Can the reason be that, somewhere deep in our subconscious, pilgrimage serves as a metaphor for life's bewildering voyage? Certainly, a characteristic of virtually every age is an unshakeable urge to seek deeper meaning and mystical resonance by travelling to some distant place which past generations have vested with enhanced spirituality and redemptive powers.

Medieval pilgrims would have needed this urge in abundance to complete the great penitential paths of their time, for in those far-off days, mechanised transport had yet to effectively kill off the concept of distance. Nevertheless, history informs us that huge numbers of these early wanderers found the motivation to follow the great redemptive trails of the Western World. They journeyed to Rome, Palestine, Canterbury, Lough Derg and the shrine of St James at Compostela in north-western Spain, along with a host of other lesser-known sites.

These arduous excursions into what must then have been a scarily unknown world have long fascinated me since they were undertaken without what have become the unquestioned modern prerequisites of travel insurance, smart phones and GPS systems. Passports were also unknown and so most pilgrims just carried a letter of credentials from a bishop or abbot establishing that they had received the sacraments before leaving and were journeying in a spirit of genuine penitence. A lucky few might possess sufficient wealth to complete their redemptive expedition on horseback or by taking passage on a ship from ports such as Venice or Southampton but mostly pilgrims just walked and walked. Counting calories was not, we can safely assume, the prime concern for these medieval sanctity seekers as they toiled on relentlessly through unmapped and often hostile lands.

Strangers journeying in strange lands, they would have been out of touch with home for up to a year and mostly in areas where people spoke indecipherable foreign tongues. Regularly, they must have felt isolated, lonely and vulnerable to robbery, kidnap and even murder. And yet, whether motivated by escaping damnation or gaining eternal reward, they persisted, driven on each day by the hope of reaching the sanctuary of a monastery or an inn and thus avoiding the dangers of spending a night in the open. And it was not just the common people who went on pilgrimage, for escaping hellfire proved a great medieval leveller. King Henry II of England undertook a redemptive journey to atone for the murder of Thomas à Becket in Canterbury Cathedral, while Holy Roman Emperor Henry IV went barefoot to the Italian town of Canossa to beg Pope Gregory VII to repeal his excommunication.

The Middle Ages were the glory years of mass pilgrimage. Indulgences didn't come cheap and there was money, power, prestige and, of course, genuine piety bound up with the penitential industry. Small wonder then, that access to pilgrim sites was considered crucially important to the Western Church and that a succession of medieval pontiffs ordered a series of bloody crusades to the Holy Land aimed at wresting back Jerusalem and the holy places from Islamic conquerors.

Historians are now as one in telling us that the coming of the Reformation represented a watershed for Western Europe by breaking forever the power of the monolithic Roman Church. To this day, the enduring impression we have of Martin Luther and his fellow reformers is that they were unswervingly sincere in their beliefs but – shall we say? – not exactly the life and soul of a party. Unsurprisingly then, this rather severe and pragmatic bunch were little given to grand gestures. Believing that salvation could more satisfactorily be accomplished at home and, perhaps, also suspecting that pilgrims might slyly try to incorporate some pleasures of the flesh into their redemptive odysseys, they immediately sent a spanner clattering into the smoothly oiled workings of the redemptive walks industry.

Expressing opposition to the idea that sins could be forgiven by a long excursion of atonement, the reformers did much to lessen the medieval tradition of faith-based redemptive travel. But in the end it was rapidly changing events that overwhelmed the pilgrim ideal. Political instability and a series of long-drawn-out wars eventually led to the virtual elimination from northern Europe of the traditional long-distance spiritual journey.

It seems, however, that the basic human yearning to seek deeper meaning from a transformational journey could not be denied for long and it eventually resurrected itself in a new wave of travel to Marian shrines that was facilitated by relatively stable political conditions in the nineteenth century and the growth of mass transportation. It all began, rather improbably, in the small and then virtually unknown French town of Lourdes in 1858. Here, reports of Marian apparitions to Bernadette Soubirous, an illiterate peasant girl, immediately brought in hordes of devotional tourists and created a welcome spending boom for this once poverty-afflicted area, which continues to the present day.

In the following years Marian apparitions in several underdeveloped areas of Europe transformed local economies: in rural Ireland, Portugal and Bosnia, with appearances at Knock in 1879, Fatima in 1917 and Medjugorje in 1981. The pilgrims that still bring badly needed spending to these locations are for the most part unswervingly devout, Roman Catholic, and solely concerned with the destination itself rather than the redemptive journey. They come in great tidal waves each summer seeking physical, spiritual and emotional healing. Unlike medieval pilgrimage, where the tradition of walking arose from necessity, modern Marian pilgrims rarely – if ever – come on foot. Instead they use trains, automobiles and planes and mostly seek comfortable accommodation in guesthouses and hotels.

The past, of course, never completely dies but sooner or later comes back to catch up with us. So the late twentieth and early twenty-first centuries have been notable for a movement away from destination-driven penitential travel towards heeding the ageless siren call of the long walk to an evocative place of sanctity. Every second walking enthusiast we meet nowadays seems to be off seeking the allure of the sacred or, perhaps, just chasing some personal goal along an ancient pilgrim path. Footing it may no longer be a necessity, but in recent years huge numbers of otherwise staunchly pragmatic people have suddenly come down with pilgrim-trail fever. In many ways the journey itself has now become the objective; the sought-after personal renewal comes not so much from the destination as from the walk itself. People search for the elusive butterfly of fulfilment and self-awareness by heading for Iona in Scotland, Canterbury in England and along the Via Francigena to Rome. Above all else, however, they are discovering a New Jerusalem on the Camino or Way of St James – a fishing net of paths all leading to Santiago de Compostela in northern Spain.

Having never previously completed a pilgrim trail for redemptive reasons, I have, nonetheless, pondered for some time their startlingly increased popularity in modern times. Are pilgrims discovering their two feet once again, as many would have us believe, for deeply spiritual reasons? Or do they merely wish to appreciate the true scale of the landscape and the immense simplification of life that comes with long-distance walking? Then, at the destination, do they feel some profoundly rewarding but non-spiritual right to be there, which they have hard earned in blisters and sweat?

Answering these questions seems in many ways like trying to know the unknowable. Indeed, pilgrims are often unable to rationalise even their own motivation for completing a penitential path. One thing is certain, however: redemption-driven travel to Ireland has – regardless of its often-indecipherable inspiration – a long tradition. Early Christian scholars came to Clonmacnoise, medieval penitents to Lough Derg and Glendalough, while others sought heightened spirituality by visiting Skellig Michael or climbing Croagh Patrick.

But what of today? Are Ireland's pilgrim paths and sacred mountains still echoing with the footfall of those yearning for some undying truth, or on the other hand, are they merely populated by seekers of gym-slim torsos? Starting at Slieve Mish, where many believe Christianity in Ireland had its first dawning, and finishing where once the known world ended on Skellig Michael, my aim is to ramble the ancient pilgrim paths of Ireland to see if they still resonate with the mysticism of the past for 21st-century pilgrims.

1

SLIEVE MISH (SLEMISH) | County Antrim

OVERVIEW A short but enthralling route to a summit that offers dreamy views over the mythical north-east of Ireland. Croagh Patrick seems to have cornered the market as St Patrick's devotional mountain, however, for there is little to represent the reputedly strong links between this striking eminence and Ireland's national apostle.

SUITABILITY Be warned: the route described is short but quite steep in places and slippery where wet. It requires the skills of easy-grade scrambling to overcome some of the difficulties on ascent and descent, while the path is ill defined in places. Boots should be worn and walking poles could be of some help during the descent.

GETTING THERE From the Ballymena bypass take the A42 to Broughshane; Slieve Mish/Slemish is well signposted from Broughshane. The start/finish is at the car park north of Slieve Mish at D217 057.

TIME Allow a little over an hour of actual walking time to complete both ascent and descent.

DISTANCE The route is about 2km and involves an ascent of 200m.

MAP OSNI *Discoverer Series* 09 Ballymena/Larne.

When I began putting it around that I was off to explore the ancient pilgrim paths of Ireland for my next book, I knew people would find it hard to get their heads around it. Among the choice responses were 'What, you a pilgrim?', 'But that's a religious book, isn't it?', 'I didn't think we had any of those,' and 'Are you walking to Spain?'

Despite such mystified incomprehension, I soon found myself ready for the off in Belfast. And, indeed, I was glad to start my pilgrim itinerary in this youthful red-brick city compressed between hill and lough. Ever since my first visit, I have always liked this friendly but unfathomable, up-front but enigmatic, metropolis.

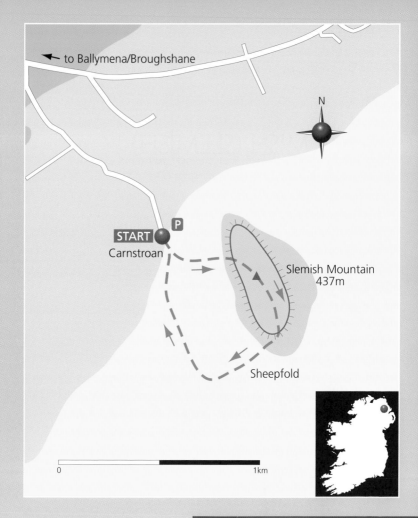

to Ballymena/Broughshane

N

START
Carnstroan

P

Slemish Mountain
437m

Sheepfold

0   1km

Slieve Mish

On my arrival, there is much hoopla about the recent opening of a huge, £97 million visitor centre aimed at rebooting Northern Irish tourism by commemorating the ill-fated *Titanic*, which was built in the Belfast shipyards. I check into the Park Inn Hotel, one of the shiny new hostelries that now populate the once-dilapidated city centre.

Bright and early next morning, as I drive north towards Northern Ireland's bible belt, it immediately strikes me how attractive but underappreciated the Ulster countryside really is. This isn't, perhaps, surprising in a province that has really only made international headlines for the renown of its writers and the doughty persistence of its urban rioters.

The Antrim hill that will forever be associated with St Patrick lies about 35 miles north of Belfast and is the focal point of an annual Patrician pilgrimage on St Patrick's Day and so it is first on my list of pilgrim routes. Acutely conscious that I am an unreconstructed sinner now following the saint's road, I switch on the car radio to distract me from this uncomforting fact. A surprisingly vehement debate is taking place on a local station about the age of the Giant's Causeway. Northern Ireland's most renowned visitor attraction and a World Heritage Site is, apparently, about to get a spanking new £18.5 million visitor centre and the discussion is going something like this: the first speaker points out that all mainstream scientific opinion holds that the causeway was formed 60 million years ago by cooling lava. 'No, it wasn't, it was created 6,000 years ago,' is the reply. 'It can't be; it's the result of a volcanic explosion and Ireland had no active volcanoes 6,000 years ago.' 'It wasn't a volcano; it was created by God when he made the world,' is the response. 'How can you be sure of that?' interjects the presenter. 'It says so in the bible, that's the infallible word of the Almighty.' 'But you can't take the bible so

Panoramic view of the basalt plug of Slieve Mish.
(Gareth McCormack)

literally. What about Jonah being swallowed by a whale and Noah building an ark big enough …' 'A whale can swallow a man if it's the will of God.' 'I feel an urge to ring the station and point out to the protagonists that they are both completely wrong. In school I remember clearly being told many times that the Giant's Causeway was built as part of a bridge to Scotland by Ireland's pre-Christian strongman, Finn McCool.

On the Ballymena bypass, the steep, unmistakeable prominence of Slieve Mish – called Slemish on maps – is obvious to my right. Initially, taking the A42 to Broughshane and then following the directional signs, I note the neatly appointed, prosperous-looking farms, which always appear to contrast strongly with the south, where many farmsteads seem to wallow in a permanent state of benign neglect.

Eventually I fetch up at the trailhead car park. Whether they believe the Giant's Causeway arose from volcanic action 60 million years ago or was created by the Almighty six millennia ago, Slieve Mish is undoubtedly popular among local people – there are ramblers and family groups already either heading to or returning from the summit. I get little sense, however, that it was from here the spark was ignited that ultimately sent the Christian message sweeping across Ireland. There are no repentant pilgrims in evidence, no stalls selling St Patrick statues, no hazel sticks for rent. Instead, everyone seems focused on exercise or leisure and not at all overawed by the fact that they are following in the footsteps of the world's most renowned national apostle.

In truth, of course, the early life story of Patrick is almost impenetrably hazy, based mainly on stories and mythologies. According to tradition, Patrick was the son of a wealthy Roman Christian in Britain. In AD 401, at the age of a sixteen, he was captured and sold into slavery to Milchu, a landowner residing in Antrim's Braid Valley. Perhaps he first came to understand the powerful symbolism of high places when he worked for six years as a herdsman on the slopes of Slieve Mish. In any case, he experienced a profound religious epiphany while tending flocks, which compelled him to alter his destiny. He came to believe God was calling him to convert the Irish people to Christianity. This motivated him to escape from Ireland and in later years return as a bishop and missionary.

One of the best known Patrician mythologies holds that soon after his arrival back in Ireland, Patrick, with heroic indifference to the rituals of royalty, defied Laoghaire, the High King of Ireland, by ascending the Hill of Slane and lighting the first Pascal fire in advance of Laoghaire's lighting of the Bealtaine fire on the Hill of Tara. Surprising as it may seem, this apparently petty and foolhardy act of defiance had the effect of igniting a bush fire that raced with the speed of a tsunami across Ireland.

View from the summit of Slieve Mish over the main car park and visitor centre.

So impressed was Laoghaire by Patrick's audacity that he immediately allowed him a free hand to carry the Christian message throughout the length and breadth of Ireland.

So Patrick went on his missionary way and soon after was scrambling up the Rock of Cashel to baptise the King of Munster, while also reputedly finding time to establish a monastery atop Ardpatrick hill in County Limerick. Tradition also holds that he blessed a well after spending a night high in the Maumturk Mountains and finally that he fasted for forty days on Croagh Patrick's summit.

In those days, people walked only out of necessity and Patrick would not have undertaken these ascents lightly or for leisure purposes. He clearly understood the powerful imagery associated with the most elevated locations, and was aware of their unmatched ability to evoke the necessary reverence and awe required to reinforce the impact of his message.

If he lived today it would be easy to imagine modern-day management experts breaking into jargon to describe him as a 'charismatic change-agent and transformational leader, who succeeded by using reverence for high places to position a user-friendly and well-targeted belief system in a pagan society'.

It is, of course, almost inconceivable that St Patrick was the first Christian missionary to Ireland in the way it is unlikely that Christopher Columbus was the first European to reach America. After all, the Roman Empire had been Christianised for over a century before Patrick, and Ireland had strong trade links with Roman Britain. Nevertheless, a simple narrative is often the most effective: the early Irish Church cannily rescued Patrick from obscurity and, in a series of hagiographies, credited the saint alone with converting Ireland to Christianity. So, while other missionaries have long been forgotten, Ireland's apostle lives on as one of the world's best-known, most commemorated and commercially exploited saints.

Initially, the Slieve Mish path leads upwards at a sympathetic angle. Soon, however, the smooth grasslands are behind and I find myself scrambling skywards over disobliging basalt but the advantage of a steep gradient is, however, that height comes rapidly. Unlike a Kerry hill, where an ascent that appears like an hour invariably takes two, Slieve Mish relents with surprising ease. Having mentally estimated an hour to the top, I then take silly pleasure in the fact that I am on the summit plateau in half that time. Swinging right along the broad whaleback eminence, I reach the bare stones of the summit and marvel at the magnificent 360-degree views with the sleeping giant of Cave Hill lying sentinel above Belfast Lough to the south. Northwards is the great sweep of the Antrim plateau and beyond Ireland's most evocative coastline is the gleam of the ancient Sea of Moyle. This is where the Children of Lir reputedly spent 300 years, having been transformed into swans by – you guessed it – a wicked stepmother, before her spell was broken by the arrival of Christianity, brought by – no need to guess this time – St Patrick. It is a timeless vista bounded by the misty outline of distant Scottish mountains. Here, although you would find it hard to believe, I am standing at the heart of Ireland's second most populated county. And yet, all I need is a small stretch of the imagination and pre-Christian farmers are once again tending their flocks in the valleys below.

Atop some ageless stones I sit back and allow time to drift by in slow motion – as Patrick may have done on sunny days more than a millennium and a half previously. Perhaps it was in a moment such as this that he experienced his mystical epiphany. But God is apparently otherwise engaged, for there is to be no 'road to Damascus' moment for me.

I do conclude, though, that Slieve Mish is not in any sense a pilgrim destination and that Croagh Patrick has clearly established itself as the market leader with regard to Patrician tourism. Apart from a very brief description of St Patrick's association with Slieve Mish on a storyboard in the car park, the mountain lacks the summit shrine that would offer a necessary focal point for a redemptive journey. Perhaps this isn't surprising, for many believe St Patrick spent his Irish captivity not in Antrim but in North Mayo. But then, the Camino pilgrim route brings hundreds of thousands of walkers to Spain each year in honour of St James even though there is no evidence whatsoever that the saint ever visited the Iberian Peninsula during his lifetime.

Then it occurs to me that if this iconic hill were located somewhere in the south of Ireland, and not in the deepest heartland of non-conformist Ulster, somebody would surely have lugged up at least a Holy Year cross by now and, perhaps, also a statue of St Patrick, hands raised in magisterial blessing. As it is, however, my only company on the summit is a family group and a few power walkers who sashay past with 'miles away' stares while safely cocooned from the world by their iPods.

Eventually, the call back to the twenty-first century becomes too strong to ignore. Rousing myself reluctantly, I continue west with the lordly Sperrin Mountains dominating the skyline. Where the plateau disappears into a steep, rocky descent, I swing right and downhill to follow a precipitous and informal track that again demands some scrambling skills to ensure a safe descent. Once back on the lush, green sward, however, the going becomes straightforward and enjoyable. Now it is just a question of savouring the unseasonably warm early summer sunshine on the short ramble back to the car park.

2

LOUGH DERG | County Donegal

OVERVIEW In the best pilgrim tradition, this route is far removed from roads, houses and other signs of modern life and has many echoes of its pilgrim past along the way. This makes it a great way of escaping the present for a few hours without the inconvenient effort of climbing to a mountaintop.

SUITABILITY Easy route following well-maintained forest tracks with nothing that could really be referred to as a hill along the way. No special hillwalking skills required while following pleasant paths well suited for casual ramblers.

GETTING THERE From Pettigoe, which lies on the Fermanagh/ Donegal border, follow the R233. This leads directly to Station Island pier (G091 739) where pilgrims are processed before travelling by boat to Station Island.

TIME About 3 hours.   **DISTANCE** 12km approx.

MAP OSi *Discovery Series* 11 – but you won't need it as the route is clearly marked.

It is sometimes said that paradise is likely to prove disappointingly non-exclusive because everyone ultimately wants to go there. The first thing I discover on arrival at the suitably isolated Lough Derg Reception Centre is that purgatory is also a startlingly popular 21st-century destination. People are not only queuing to go, they are also busy using the self-service check-in machines to speed up their arrival at what is generally regarded as the toughest redemptive exercise in Christendom.

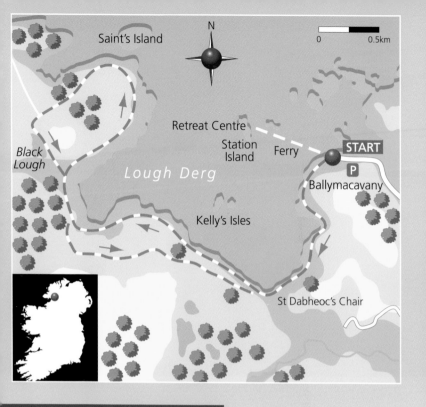

Saint's Island

N

0   0.5km

Retreat Centre

Station
Island   Ferry

START

P

Ballymacavany

Black
Lough

Lough Derg

Kelly's Isles

St Dabheoc's Chair

Lough Derg

Since medieval times the mystical call for pilgrimage to Lough Derg has never subsided. Outside, the present-day keepers of the flame are a group of mostly young adults, some of whom look as if they might have strayed in from a fashion shoot for casually elegant glamour. Instead, they have journeyed here while already fasting since midnight and are now waiting patiently in line for a boat to take them to the austere, Alcatraz-like buildings on Station Island that house St Patrick's Purgatory. Here, their holiday weekend will be spent without such modern indulgences as mobile phones, iPads or MP3 players, as they partake of a full-on, no-holds-barred spiritual makeover. Exactly as penitents from past generations have done, they will, with barefoot prayer, fasting and sleep deprivation, 'renounce the world, the flesh and the Devil' on an island once considered so remote that to travel any further would literally have involved walking off the existing maps.

The modern cross marking the embarkation point for Saint's Island.

They all seem so insouciantly stoical as they wait around – so serenely untroubled about a much-hyped pop concert in Dublin, so free of nagging doubts about missing the hectic hedonism of the Galway Races or the best party somewhere else – that for one mad moment I am tempted to renounce my misspent youth and join them. But, fortunately for all concerned, duty calls. As they have their tickets electronically scanned for boarding, I head in the other direction to pursue the ancient medieval pilgrim route that once brought penitents from across Europe to this spartan Donegal shoreline.

By the twelfth century, a cave on Lough Derg, known as St Patrick's Purgatory, had become a renowned place of pilgrimage and one of the very few Irish locations denoted on early European maps. The majority of pilgrims would come through England and then land on Ireland's east coast. From here they would have walked for close to two weeks on their redemptive trek across the Irish countryside. The final part of their journey leading to the lakeside opposite Saint's Island has now been recreated as a pilgrim path starting from the modern embarkation point for Station Island.

Following the waymarkers from here, I immediately meet a well-surfaced forest roadway skirting Lough Derg which provides occasional dreamy views across the waters to the buildings on the penitential island. I had always associated St Bridget with County Kildare but apparently she is a lady who got around a bit. Never destined, it seems, to just settle down with a man prepared to do his share of the washing-up and live happily ever after, she instead took upon herself the task of travelling across Ireland, converting people to Christianity.

First to capture my curiosity sufficiently to justify a small diversion is a viewing point denoted as St Bridget's Chair, which consists of a large, smooth rock on the water's edge. Further on there is another sign pointing this time to St Dabheoc's Chair. Dabheoc was reputedly the founder of the abbey on Saint's Island, so I feel an obligation to explore his seating place. Initially an uncooperative track leads me to a fence at the edge of a field, where, in the absence of further signs, I scramble around looking for an edifice resembling a chair. Then, on impulse, I ascend a small hill to my right and here I am rewarded with splendid views over the still waters of the lough and a rough pile of rocks that could just about be regarded as a rudimentary seat. This, I surmise, is where St Dabheoc contemplated.

Panoramic view of Station Island.

Soon after, the modern route joins the old pilgrimage trail that once conveyed medieval atonement seekers on the final leg of their transcendental journey from Templecarne Church in Pettigoe. Following in the ghostly footsteps of these early penitents, it is easy to imagine their weary rejoicing at the first sight of Lough Derg before they continued along this lonesome Donegal shoreline and then crossed the now long-vanished wooden bridge to the Augustinian abbey on Saint's Island.

St Bridget remains second only to Patrick in popularity among Irish saints and soon I come upon yet another shrine in her honour. Offering absorbing views across the lake, this is clearly a genuine place of pilgrimage, for a cross marks the site and the surrounding trees are richly adorned with favours and votive offerings.

So far so meditative, but now a pile of logs to one side of the track suggests that forest harvesting operations are in progress. And sure enough, a low steel gate soon bars the route, accompanied by a warning stating: 'No unauthorised persons beyond this point'. This begs the question: are pilgrims properly 'authorised persons' and does this mean that faux pilgrims like myself merely writing about pilgrim routes are also vicariously authorised? I have no idea about the answer to this question, but still can't help wondering what early pilgrims did when they encountered a sign stating 'trespassers will be beheaded' or 'boiled in oil' or indeed whatever the medieval equivalent of a 'no entry' sign was.

Deciding, however, that fortitude will surely bring its own reward, I resolve to push ahead. After all, medieval pilgrims surely faced far greater dangers; besides, I can see that the route ahead is free of further obstructions. So I bravely leap this 2ft-high forest Rubicon and continue as the route gradually swings north by the lakeshore and traverses an increasingly remote landscape to reach the headland opposite Saint's Island. This is marked by a simple, modern cross, but nothing now remains of the monastery where penitents spent a couple of weeks in penance and spiritual preparation before being rowed across for a 24-hour redemptive vigil in the cave on Station Island. Saint's Island ultimately fell victim to the sixteenth-century dissolution of the monasteries and, from then on, pilgrims went directly from the shoreline to the cave site. There remains, however, a resonance of deeper meaning about the place, which makes it as far removed from the materialistic world of the present day as it was in medieval times. It seems a wonderful setting to just sit back and reconnect with nature and the spiritual world. I sit there, enveloped by tranquility, and immediately cannot help wondering why we haven't recreated the original pilgrim route to Lough Derg from Ireland's east coast in the style of the Spanish Camino.

Too soon the time comes when I must take my leave of the medieval past and continue by circling further the serene lakeshore. Eventually, the waymarkers veer inland and take me past the lonely curl of water that forms tiny Black Lough before rejoining my outward route. Now it is just a question of retracing my steps to the Station Island pier. Here, in further proof that the past never truly goes away, pilgrims in a slightly older age bracket have arrived and are queuing in no-nonsense attire to reject the modern world and live, for a time, the life of a medieval penitent. Uncomfortably aware that I'm not a true pilgrim and don't really belong among these admirably unmaterialistic redemption seekers, I carry my rucksack back to the car where a new arrival inquires, 'how was the pilgrimage for you?' 'I had a great time at Lough Derg,' is my truthful reply.

3

SLIEVE LEAGUE | County Donegal

OVERVIEW Height is gained reasonably easily to the church ruins and holy well located above Lough Agh. This is followed by an obligatory crossing of One Man's Pass to gain the summit, which is often billed as the Becher's Brook of the ascent. In reality it should present few difficulties for even moderately experienced walkers as the drops on both sides are far from vertical and not particularly alarming.

NOTE Slieve League has in recent years become a classic example of a superb scenic spectacle devalued by its own popularity. This has led to considerable erosion on the mountainside. Walkers wishing to enjoy the spectacular cliff-top scenery are, therefore, requested to either ascend or return via the Pilgrim's Path to reduce erosion and crowding on the route from Bunglass.

SUITABILITY The Pilgrim Path on Slieve League is a moderately challenging walk mostly on track with an altitude gain of about 450m and is suitable for most moderately experienced ramblers. From the summit, walkers have the option to retrace their steps or to choose instead the steeper but more scenic route along the cliff top to Bunglass. If the latter option is taken, those not used to scrambling should avoid the steep rock rib beyond Keeringear by traversing left and taking the path that circles this obstacle on the inland side of the ridge.

Walkers should also be aware that Slieve League is exposed to sudden weather changes from the Atlantic and requires boots, waterproof clothing and a packed lunch. Some navigation skills may be needed on a misty day when traversing the plateau prior to crossing One Man's Pass.

It is also important to arrange for a pickup if you decide on a descent to Bunglass. Otherwise you are unlikely to appreciate the 7km road walk at the end of a reasonably challenging day that will be necessary to recover your vehicle from above Teelin.

GETTING THERE From Donegal town follow the N56 west to Killybegs and then take the R263 to Carrick. From there, go south for approximately 2km and then swing right along a byroad that is signposted for Slieve League Pilgrim Path. Continue following the signs through a gateway until you reach a small parking lot beyond which further access by mechanised transport is prohibited.

HIGHEST ALTITUDE Slieve League summit (595m).

TIME Allow about 3.5 hours for a there-and-back ascent via the Pilgrim Path. Add another hour if you decide to descend to Bunglass.

DISTANCE About 7km (whether you choose a there-and-back ascent via the Pilgrim Path, or the descent to Bunglass).

MAP OSi *Discovery Series* 10.

The Pilgrim Path ascending Slieve League.

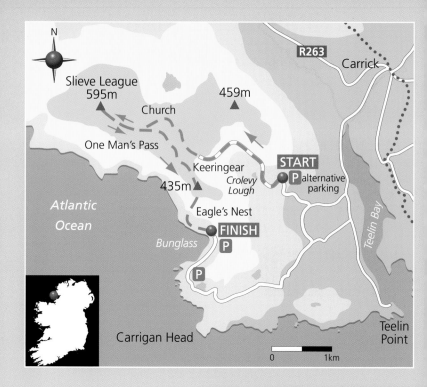

A quirk of the Irish personality is a fondness for moving statues, milky tea and maintaining a standing position when drinking in pubs. Another of our idiosyncrasies is a strong attachment to bungalows arranged in extended ribbon developments along our roadsides.

Donegal offers many fine examples of this latter un-endearing national tendency and so, as I rove west through the county on a sunny summer morning, it is perhaps unsurprising that there are many grossly elongated villages along the way. Then in the village of Teelin, I swing right from the coast road and suddenly all of Ireland's irresponsibility with concrete blocks in sublime countryside is forgotten. With the familiar little pulse of excitement that always comes with exploring a new route, I head into the remote, fairy-tale fastness of the Slieve League Mountains.

When a sign points left for the Slieve League Pilgrim Path, I park carefully while making sure not to block access for those going up the laneway or to a nearby gateway. Having grabbed my rucksack, I am just leaving when a car comes by and a lady driver rolls down her window. 'Are you thinking of parking here?' she enquires. This seems very much

The Slieve League cliffs as seen from Bunglass.

like a loaded question, right out of the days when landowners and walkers were at severe loggerheads. It is also a difficult query to answer sensibly for obviously I am 'thinking of parking here'. That's exactly why I have just locked the car and am about to head up the mountain. I gaze around to see if there is any way I could conceivably be in someone's way and conclude that there is not. So I reply that 'yes, I am', and wait to be informed of some reason why this is antisocial, immoral, outrageous or whatever. Instead, she says, 'you can save yourself a long walk by driving up further and parking in the car park at the end of the lane.'

Whether she genuinely has my interests at heart or is simply concerned others will follow my example but park less considerately, I have no idea. In any case, it is good news for me. So I thank her for the information and then rousing my horseless carriage to further effort, I continue up the well-surfaced lane and go through a gate to reach a nicely laid-out parking lot.

Slieve League, along with Croagh Patrick and Mount Brandon, forms a trinity of sacred but once very remote mountains lying close to Ireland's west coast. For over a thousand years the monastic site close to Slieve

League's summit was a focus for Christian pilgrims who took the line of least resistance upwards from Teelin.

Following in their footsteps from my parking place, I find it pleasant going as I pile on up the firm pathway past lonesome Croleavy Lough to reach a modern footbridge constructed beneath a scenic waterfall. Here a couple of families are celebrating one of the few good days of summer by dipping their feet in the crystal-clear pools. I pause awhile to take in my surroundings, with my eyes being drawn to walkers on the much busier route up from Bunglass as they pass over the stark outline of Keeringear Mountain.

Eventually, the tortuous path dribbles out near the objective for early Christian penitents. This isolated monastic site still holds the forlorn remains of a chapel along with the ruins of some stone huts and a nearby spring whose waters are – most usefully for a mountaintop location – reputed to offer a cure for aching joints.

It is something of a mystery to me why anyone would choose to set up a monastery on this austere, storm-lashed Donegal plateau or how these holy men managed to survive when surrounded by such unproductive land. I don't know the answer to this but it is apparent that these early monks were hardy, unmaterialistic souls. Ultimately, they abandoned Slieve League but not, as you might expect, in favour of some fertile well-watered lowland abbey. Incapable, it seems, of settling for a comfortable retirement, they sallied forth from nearby Teelin Bay and, with messianic zeal, carried the Christian message in their tiny boats across the cruel North Atlantic Ocean. Reaching the even more inhospitable shores of Iceland after many adventures, they then apparently Christianised the local inhabitants.

Next, I follow a muddle of cairns across a plateau to join the cliff-top path and then swing right along the edge. To reach the summit, it is now necessary to traverse the rather overdramatised One Man's Pass. This turns out to be nothing more than an elevated but well-trodden path a metre wide and about 300m in length.

The summit is a little disappointing. Crowned by a broken trig pillar, it is really just a continuation of the ridge and doesn't truly have the feel of a distinct mountaintop. The compensation, however, is an inspirational vista stretching from the eye-watering whiteness of Errigal on the northern horizon to the unmistakable eminence of Yeats' famous Ben Bulben, far away to the south.

Retracing my steps across One Man's Pass, I continue descending the cliff-top path to Bunglass rather than go back down the Pilgrim Route. I had been up and down this route before but had forgotten that one more obstacle barred my descent. I am on it before I see it, a narrow rib of rock descending from Keeringear summit with alarming drops on either side.

My trump card here is familiarity. I have met this obstacle before and know that, while it looks intimidating, it is actually rather benign, offering plenty of security in the form of large, user-friendly handholds. Ahead of me a girl sashays down the rib effortlessly while her boyfriend seems to have seriously misjudged his capacities as he struggles to stay in control. Safely off the rock she begins to tease his ineptitude as he, shivering, clings to the crest. Apparently, she has no intention of sallying up to his rescue, despite the fact that their relationship could terminate abruptly at any moment in a 400m descent to the unforgiving rocks below. Not wishing to dwell too long on the consequences of such an occurrence, I begin suggesting where he might place his hands and feet for security. He seems grateful for this intervention and thus we continue down with intermittent cries of 'come on, you wimp,' ringing from below.

Once safely back on terra firma, as it were, the young man thanks me for my advice and I feel constrained to point out, rather sportingly I thought, that this rock rib is always a pretty scary descent the first time you do it. His girlfriend is not to be mollified, however. 'Ah, there's nothing to it,' she says, 'sure I'd never done it before either. I'd have done Carrauntoohil long ago, too, if he wasn't so hopeless.' Soon after, they nonchalantly head on down the mountain leaving me a little lost for words and acutely perplexed by the curious nature of so many human relationships.

Following them, I enjoy many stroll-stopping views traversing the startlingly sheer vistas from above the almost visceral beauty of what are billed Europe's highest and most dramatic sea cliffs. I take a short break to absorb the scenery at the monumentally elevated viewing point of The Eagles Nest, before descending along a more heavily eroded part of the track and eventually reaching a paved section with a handrail. Immediately, a crush of humanity thickens like a forest around me.

Slieve League is undoubtedly one of the big beasts of Irish upland tourism and when I finally arrive at its topmost car park, it immediately reminds me of O'Connell Street in Dublin on the morning of an All-Ireland hurling final. The place is hopelessly overcrowded. People are milling around in all directions as if not too clear what exactly to do with themselves until the match starts.

Sometimes it is said, with unswerving accuracy, that where there's a will there's a relative. I will now add to this that where there's a crowd there's an entrepreneur or two and so I now purchase a bottle of water from one of the ice cream vans, which are doing a brisk trade. Then, as the evening sunshine turns the great cliffs a startling shade of crimson while silvering the ocean below, I settle down to wait for the arrival of my lift back to the pilgrim trail car park above Teelin. Immediately, I notice the couple encountered earlier on the Keeringear rock rib. They are sitting arm in arm on a nearby wall and romantically sharing an ice cream cone.

Author's note: there are two candidates for the title One Man's Pass on Slieve League. The first is the easy arête about 300m long, which is crossed to reach the summit. This is marked 'One Man's Pass' on OSi maps. The other candidate is the rock rib atop the cliffs near Keeringear summit, which is a more formidable challenge and is favoured by many local people. In general OSi maps have been used as the final arbiter with regards to place names in this book. So, pending the emergence of a consensus on this issue and to avoid confusion, it has been decided to accept the current OSi denomination regarding the location of One Man's Pass.

4

TURAS COLMCILLE | County Donegal

OVERVIEW There is little doubt that Turas Colmcille remains a genuine and unsanitised pilgrim route undertaken in the main for devotional reasons, for it is difficult to imagine anyone wanting to complete this tough circuit just for pleasure.

The pilgrimage starts from the Protestant chapel and proceeds past several stations to Beefan, the most westerly point on the route. From Beefan, the pilgrims descend Mullach na Cainte, traditionally the only place along the route where pilgrims are allowed to talk. The route then leads through a marsh (The Umar Dubh) and after several more stations returns to the start point by the banks of the Murlin River, before crossing this river on large stepping stones to return to the Church of Ireland chapel.

The organised Turas pilgrimage occurs on 9 June each year, the feast day of St Colmcille. Historically, it was performed by barefoot pilgrims leaving at midnight. This tradition of barefoot pilgrimage continues to the present day.

SUITABILITY The route lies entirely within the Glencolumbkille Valley. Route-finding difficulties and marshy terrain makes traversing the floor of the glen problematic, to say the least. Also, crossing fences and stone walls presents difficulties as there are almost no stiles on the route. Walkers completing the full route need to be well equipped with waterproof clothing and sturdy boots and to be aware that walkers have experienced difficulties in the marshiest sections and have had to be assisted by locals.

For those intending to complete the Turas in its entirety, it is probably best to join one of the periodic organised pilgrimages or else employ the services of a local guide. Details of those who provide this service are available from Oideas Gael Glencolumbkille: (353) (0)74 97 30 248; email; eolas@oideas-gael.com.

Otherwise it is certainly easier, and not much further, for pilgrims to retrace their steps from Station 8 and continue to Station 9 by road. The final section of the Turas also traverses very rough, vegetated terrain along the banks of the Murlin River. Here, it might again be advisable to retrace the route from Station 14 and return by road to Station 15 at the Church of Ireland chapel.

GETTING THERE From Donegal town follow the N56 west to Killybegs and then take the R263 to Glencolumbkille. The Turas starts and finishes beside the Church of Ireland chapel at Glencolumbkille (G534 850).

DISTANCE About 5km. **TIME** Allow at least 3 hours to complete.

MAP OSi *Discovery Series* 10.

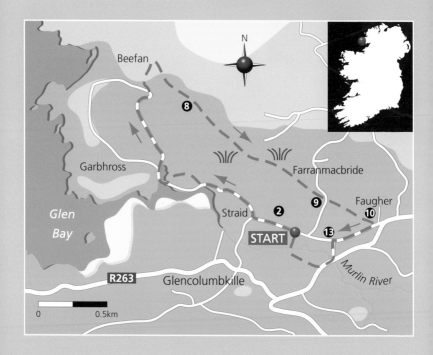

St Columba's Church of Ireland chapel at Glencolumbkille.

At this moment, following the Irish pilgrim trails feels like the most compelling endeavour in the world. I am heading through the wild, sun-kissed Donegal highlands towards a once-impoverished area that was, nevertheless, a magnet for medieval penitents. Indeed, whenever I feel nostalgia for the vanished landscapes of youth my thoughts inevitably turn to the place where I once enjoyed a wonderfully lazy, hazy few weeks masquerading as a student of the Irish language.

I am looking forward to revisiting Glencolumbkille after a twenty-year absence. It was then, by any standards, a remote location and it is perhaps for this reason that the Irish language and a vibrant Gaelic culture survived here. The area was also justifiably renowned as the parish made famous by Fr James McDyer who championed the rights of rural people and helped establish community-based enterprises in the area.

Having crossed the marvellously bleak, black bogs beyond Carrick, my descent into Glencolumbkille is, as always, breathtaking with the defiant green valley laid out in resolute isolation below. Now long-forgotten memories come flooding back. Through sepia-tinted spectacles I can, once again, see our little group ambling light-heartedly to classes and the odd evening céilí along the grass that grew in abundance in the middle of traffic-untroubled roads. In this idyllic, rustic backwater it was only very occasionally necessary to give way to an ancient Massey Ferguson or a battered Ford Escort.

In his renowned Irish travelogue, *The Way that I Went*, Robert Lloyd Praeger wrote: 'in the sixth century, St Columba journeyed over miles of moorland with a band of disciples to find this sequestered valley shut in between mountains and the ocean, a spot meant for meditation and prayer.' At the age of twenty-five, Columba (confusingly, also known as Colmcille), a man of seemingly boundless energy, is reputed to have already founded twenty-seven monasteries across Ireland. Later, he travelled on one of the first pilgrim journeys out of the country, carrying with him the Christian message or what, I guess, would in the information age be termed a knowledge-based export. He went on to establish a monastery at Iona in Scotland and to convert most of the country to Christianity. Modern management theorists would probably refer to him as the perfect 9.9 leader – hugely endowed with people skills to inspire the unswerving devotion of his followers while still managing to get an enormous number of tasks accomplished.

Unsurprisingly then, his name, rather than that of Patrick, is ubiquitous, in the valley. And, of course, it is easy to see why Columba would have chosen the valley, now named in his honour, as a place for his monastery, for it has contemplative life written all over it, offering an isolated location in a fertile valley. My objective for visiting the glen is to complete the Turas Colmcille, which consists mostly of standing stones of pagan origin that had crosses carved into them in the early Christian period. These have then been knotted together adroitly in a redemptive sequence to facilitate those wishing to complete the Stations of the Cross.

It's the height of the tourist season and Glencolumbkille is certainly busier than I remember it. In the car park opposite the Fr McDyer Folk Village, which lies directly beside an impossibly pretty beach, a half dozen coaches and innumerable cars are already in occupation, forcing me up

Looking across Glen Bay towards Glen Head, which is topped by a tower, overlooking Glencolumbkille.

the road to park. In the souvenir shop I purchase a pocket guide entitled *Turas Colmcille*, which describes the pilgrim route within the valley and I also obtain a map from the lady at the checkout.

When I notice that the route shown on the map inexplicably disappears abruptly around the seventh station and point this out to the lady at the till, she replies, 'It's a pilgrimage, you see: you've got to find your own way through the marsh.'

I am in no hurry for clearly this will be one of my easier days. From the map I can see that the route is nearby and lies entirely within the Glencolumbkille Valley. So I head down the road and call in for a leisurely coffee to the well-appointed headquarters of the renowned Oideas Gael, an institute established in 1984 to promote the Irish language and culture that now offers language learning and walking holidays, among many other pursuits. The woman at reception tells me that the Turas Colmcille has fifteen stations in all, including Colmcille's Chapel, a wishing stone and a holy well, adding, 'you'll need boots to do the full circuit for it gets pretty marshy.'

Station 9, Glencolumbkille.

In my guidebook, the Turas is billed as beginning from the nineteenth-century St Columba's Church of Ireland chapel. It stands, dignified and unpretentious, a short distance from the village centre. Here I dither for a while, looking around for the first station. In the graveyard surrounding the church I come upon a mysterious wooden trapdoor. Could the first station actually be located underground? It isn't, but later I discover the trapdoor conceals something interesting: beneath is a large Iron Age souterrain, discovered accidentally when a grave was being dug in 1832. It contains a roomy central chamber and metre-high tunnels running east and west, which, of course, proves the church is built on the site of a much earlier settlement. A local man, with the kind but worn face of one who has lived through many an Atlantic storm, sees my predicament and points out the first station and tells me the Turas is a great circuit but 'for you rather than me'. When I enquire what he means he replies rather vaguely as he heads away. 'It's just the boggy bits I don't like. You know, people often get stuck down there.' All this talk of marshes and bogs reminds me of no less a personage then Sherlock Holmes and his Dartmoor adventures in *The Hound of the Baskervilles*.

Soon, however, I am on the Turas and heading off jauntily through a landscape heavy with Christianised megalithic tombs, standing stones and cairns. The first station, Straid burial tomb, is followed closely by the second: a cross-inscribed pillar. Up the road and beyond a bridge, the trail goes right. Station three is known as Garvecross Cairn, and then a little further on I come upon station four, the Beefan Cross Pillar, and number five, St Colmcille's Chapel. The route undoubtedly weaves a mystical spell for I notice how busy it is with visitors as I am drawn out onto open hillside and begin ascending past Colmcille's Chair where the saint is reputed to have rested. Here, I am surprised to meet several groups walking down towards me as though they have abandoned the Turas but gamely I press on.

Eventually I arrive at Colmcille's Well, which is protected on three sides by a large cairn and is adorned with favours and small pieces of bric-a-brac, left as offerings by pilgrims past. Above me, walkers continue towards a cliff-top Napoleonic-era signal tower. These coastal towers were built in a time of extreme paranoia, when it was believed that a small man with a big hat was about to turn all of Europe into one nation state. From past experience I know the tower offers a sensational viewing point, but resolutely sticking to my knitting, I descend instead in a south-easterly direction as indicated by the Turas map. Now it becomes obvious why so many have turned back, for the track has disappeared and the bouldery, heathery slopes make for hard going in the best unsanitised pilgrim tradition.

There are no directional arrows and finding Station 8 turns out to be a tough ask. Eventually, by comparing a photograph in my guidebook with the contours of the hillside above, I come upon an unimpressive stone-built enclosure. Conscious that all this flapping around is taking something of the shine out of my day, I investigate Station 8 and find it consists of three cairns and two standing stones. From here my guidebook tells me that 'pilgrims cross Umar Ghlinne (the trough of the glen)' but also goes on to warn that 'the path is ill defined and visitors may prefer to retrace their steps back to the roadway.'

With, perhaps, overabundant self-regard, I immediately slot myself into the category of a 21st-century Colmcille and boldly strike out across the marsh. This immodest self-delusion proves my undoing for instantly I sink ignominiously a few feet into a reedy swamp. Extracting my now mucky self with some difficulty, I try another route and end up being headed off by deep drainage channels and then by a fence and eventually I end up mired in more marshy ground. Apparently a pilgrim track does exist through the marsh but try as I might, I can't find it.

One thing I do know, however, is that rocks don't remain on the surface in boggy terrain. Away to the left I spot some large boulders and strike out in this direction. Here at least it is possible to remain above the coarse grass as I cross an area of rough terrain to join a rustic lane near a picturesque, thatched cottage. I follow this lane to reach a tarmac road which soon afterwards swings back right towards the village at a road junction.

Station 9, 'the gathering stone', lies immediately right of this road and consists of a standing stone with a hole cut through it. Referring to my guidebook I learn that those in a state of grace will get a glimpse of heaven through this opening. Hopefully, I put my eye to the aperture, expecting pearly gates and winged angels serenading the righteous with golden harps, but am rewarded only with the dark brooding background of a pine forest.

Disappointed, I cross the road and continue through a gate, a wood and a field to reach the next station, which consists of an undecorated slab beside a modern bungalow. Clambering over another fence, I join a road and pass two more stations in the form of standing stones to reach Station 13 inharmoniously sited at a T-junction beside the Garda station. Even more incongruously, it is actually a fibreglass model of an original standing stone that was damaged and removed.

Feeling that I am now on the last leg of my tough station round, I cross a bridge beyond the fibreglass model and then swing right into a no-concessions-to-vernacular-architecture housing estate. Scrambling over yet another fence I encounter more rough terrain by the riverbank. Eventually I fetch up at the fourteenth station, a cairn upon which rests a slender standing stone with an ornate design. The decoration here, apparently, is typical of its period and shows that Glencolumbkille was in early Christian times not as remote as we might now consider, but was in contact with other centres of Christianity across these islands.

By my reckoning, this should have been the end of my Turas – there are only fourteen Stations of the Cross, right? – but Glencolumbkille has one last vegetated sting in its extended pilgrim trail for I must now cross the Murlin River on stepping stones to reach the fifteenth and final station beside the Church of Ireland chapel.

Crossing the river is not a major problem, but beyond I find no discernible path and must force my way through an egregious thicket of reeds, ferns and briars as pilgrims past must have so often been obliged to do. I am now conscious of cutting a very peculiar sight indeed to the group of tourists taking photographs by the Church of Ireland chapel, but I battle on.

After what seems an interminable ordeal – or an authentic pilgrim experience, depending on your point of view – I reach a gateway leading to a car park opposite the Church of Ireland chapel. Conscious that the tourists are still eyeing me curiously, wondering perhaps if there is an asylum across the river from which there has just been a breakout, I finally cross the road and find the last station in the church graveyard. I now feel like shouting out for their benefit, 'I have completed Turas Colmcille', but I force myself to desist. Instead I sink to my knees, not so much in prayer, but in thanksgiving for having survived what must surely be Ireland's, if not Christendom's, most demanding Stations of the Cross.

Author's note: Since the Turas crosses private land, it is only available for use by walkers between 9 June (the feast day of St Columbkille) and 15 August.

5

TÓCHAR PHÁDRAIG | County Mayo

OVERVIEW Ireland's nearest answer to the Camino and with the thermostat conveniently turned down. If you can complete only one Irish Pilgrim route, this is the one to do for the Tóchar Phádraig is the genuine article – a prehistoric, druidical pathway that still holds many resonances from the pagan past. Christianised by St Patrick, it remains stubbornly untamed and much as it was for medieval pilgrims.

SUITABILITY A long but low-level walk that is generally well waymarked but there are some tough, unsanitised, underfoot conditions in places. Attains an altitude of almost 500m on Croagh Patrick.

GETTING THERE From Castlebar, go south on the N84 for approx. 14km to reach the start point at Ballintubber Abbey (M153 779). Here you must register for the Tóchar walk. At the time of going to press, this cost €10.

FINISH Car park at Murrisk (L919 823).

TIME At least 10 hours. There is no public transport from Murrisk back to Ballintubber so you will either need to arrange a lift or organise a taxi.

EQUIPMENT Rain gear, trekking boots and warm clothing are essential while trainers may be useful for walking the tarmac sections beyond Aghagower. Route can be completed in one very challenging or two somewhat more leisurely days.

DISTANCE 35km.

MAP Map available from Ballintubber Abbey. OSi *Discovery Series* 30 and 38 also cover the route. Be aware, however, that at the time of writing, the OSi *Discovery Series* maps do not show the correct route of the Tóchar Phádraig as it approaches Croagh Patrick. There are also discrepancies around Killawullaun Mill, and on the final approach to Aghagower.

'Light a candle before you go, include the stranger in your group and no complaining.' With these words from Father Frank Fahey, and having paid a €10 registration fee, I have officially become a genuine Tóchar Phádraig pilgrim.

In many ways we are, of course, all pilgrims, searching daily for some sublime wisdom that offers an eternal truth to explain life's otherwise unaccountable journey. Today, however, with every second person I meet heading off to search for the spiritual along the Camino, I am resolutely bucking the trend by coming instead to County Mayo. Here I intend to complete the Tóchar Phádraig Pilgrim Trail that pre-dates the Way of St James by at least 500 years.

Earlier I had read that the Tóchar Phádraig was the royal road leading from Rathcruachan, the seat of the Kings of Connaught, to Cruachan Aille, the ancient name for Croagh Patrick, which even in pagan times was venerated as a sacred mountain. Later, after Saint Patrick is reputed to have fasted on the summit for forty days, and apparently also whiled away some of this time by driving the last snake out of Ireland, pilgrims began to follow that same road to the holy mountain. Over time, the route became known as the Tóchar Phádraig or St Patrick's Causeway. Then, when Ballintubber Abbey was built in 1216, the monks apparently saw a niche market in redemptive tourism. A hostel was put in place for pilgrims at the abbey who then traditionally embarked from here on the final section of their journey to what soon became Ireland's holiest mountain.

In the sixteenth century, the Tóchar fell into disuse and was finally abandoned when Penal laws were enacted against the Catholic religion. The first stirring in Ireland's modern pilgrim era came when the path was reopened in 1987. Father Fahey was the driving force behind the reawakening of the Tóchar Phádraig and he has continued to be instrumental in making the Tóchar Ireland's busiest, dedicated pilgrim walk.

In the abbey visitor centre, I learn that Ballintubber Abbey was once a prosperous place and held 3,000 acres of the best east Mayo land. Suppressed during the Protestant Reformation, it continued as a place of worship in Penal times and is thus the only place in Ireland where Mass has been celebrated continuously since the thirteenth century. Restoration work in the twentieth century repaired much of the abbey to near its former glory. Since then it has become a popular venue for celebrity weddings, including that of film star Pierce Brosnan.

Leaving the abbey grounds, I pass the remains of the baths where weary pilgrims once rested and bathed on their return from a barefoot

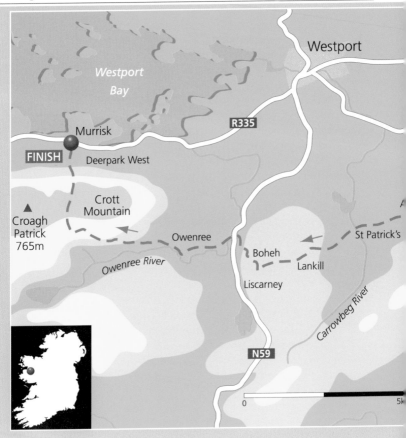

round trip to Croagh Patrick. The baths were known as the Dancora, which means 'the Bath of the Righteous' and were the place where the faithful ritually expressed a cleansing from all sin before returning to their homes with a changed heart. This acts as a reminder that medieval spiritual expeditions were – unlike today when it is almost universally considered OK for returning pilgrims to use mechanised transport – very much two-way affairs. When pilgrims reached their destination and collected their indulgences they then, somehow, had to find the motivation to face the rigours of the fatiguing plod home, all done without assistance from such modern fripperies as boots, thousand-mile socks, Gore-tex jackets and high-energy drinks.

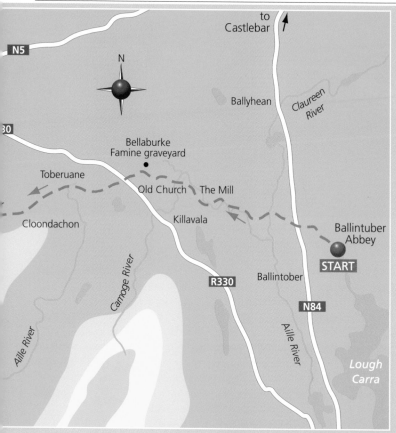

Tóchar Phádraig

In the first field, cobbled stones are still clearly exposed which were part of the ancient Tóchar. As I continue, I can't help noting that while lamentable mischief-making by past EU agricultural policies has created great dairy prairies and green deserts of monoculture in other parts, the small fields and abundant wild flowers thankfully remain along the Tóchar much as they were in ancient times when, lured by the promise of immortality, medieval pilgrims trod this selfsame trail.

Crossing a road, I enter some fields and find the underfoot conditions a little challenging, but then this is supposed to be a pilgrim trail and, unlike medieval penitents, I am comfortably shod in four-season boots. Then it's on through a landscape drenched in history and abounding with myth-

Walker setting out on the Tóchar Phádraig Pilgrim Path at Ballintubber Abbey. (Gareth McCormack)

making potential. There are stories of holy wells, priest hunters, flax mills and villages entirely obliterated by the Famine hunger.

So far so penitential, but then a thunderous sound from behind abruptly interrupts my thoughts. It's as if Charlton Heston is leading a chariot race along the Tóchar. Startled, I look behind and now realise a large herd of bullocks is hurtling towards me. This actually proves something of a relief. From an agricultural background, I know that bullocks, unlike bulls, are by nature curious but also nervous, unthreatening creatures and will be easily frightened away by a wave of my walking pole. Others might not be aware of this, which bears out the point about the unexpected challenges and dangers facing medieval pilgrims who must have been chased innumerable times and by far more threatening bulls.

A left turn now takes me over several stiles and across a footbridge to gain the N84 Galway/Castlebar Road. Crossing the road with care, it is on through Castlepark Wood, a pleasant hazel forest, to reach the Ballintubber/Killavala Road near the entrance to Lufferton House. The name Killavala is anglicised from the original Irish name *Cill an Bhealaigh* (the church of the way) and refers to the fact that a church for pilgrims was sited here in medieval times. Lufferton House, which replaced an earlier thirteenth-century castle, is reputed to have been built with stone imported from Scotland. After a short road walk, the route dives suddenly into the wildest of wild Mayo countryside. Rural and raw, it is now a series of rough fields alternating with young forest as the wandering path crosses many minor roads and streams before eventually rejoining the Ballintubber/Killavala Road.

The tenth-century round tower at Aghagower. (Gareth McCormack)

Patrician memorial at Aghagower.

Following the signs pointing left, I tag the road for about a kilometre, passing the abandoned mill at Killawullaun, which was originally built to grind both flax and corn. Just beyond a bridge the arrows point me right and cross country to the wildflower-rich banks of the Aille River, which remain much as they were in ancient times, when pilgrims passed this way in search of spiritual immortality.

When the waymarkers abandon the Aille, I climb to higher ground and am rewarded with my first 'wow' moment: standing straight ahead is Ireland's holiest and handsomest hill. Surely a moment of joyful epiphany for fatigued medieval pilgrims and today an excellent place to pause awhile and just smell the flowers. Reminding myself that life is a journey, not a destination, I reach for my lunch box and then sit and enjoy the timeless sensations and colours of the Mayo countryside. From this vantage point, Croagh Patrick reveals itself as the perfect quartzite cone, dominating the landscape with the striking lines that attract up to 20,000 penitents on the last Sunday of July each year – Reek Sunday.

It is sometimes said that Ireland has little in the way of climate but much in the way of weather. It has been a liquid summer so far and, true to form, a day that started out promisingly now becomes overcast. By the time I pass the poignant remains of a Famine graveyard at Bellaburke it has become what some would call a 'soft day', i.e. bucketing down. Repeating, but not quite convincing myself, that 'life is not about waiting for showers to pass but learning to dance in the rain,' I push ahead through fields and then left onto a minor public road.

Sod's Law ensures that I then lose the route and end up following a lane into someone's yard. A woman approaches and asks if she can help. And indeed she can, for not only does she point out the trail, she also informs me that Enda (Mayo-born Taoiseach Enda Kenny) has been hard done by in the media. As the rain continues to pour down she tells me that 'he only worked in a school down the road but people won't stop criticising him even though he is just doing his job when the country is completely broke'.

Then she wants to know who is going to win the match. Adroitly I reply, 'Mayo, I guess', even though I have no idea about their next Gaelic football match. She looks disappointed by this and tells me she thinks Ireland have a great chance of doing well against Italy in an upcoming soccer game. Then referring to some recent Irish defeats, she claims that if only Trapattoni (Ireland's football manager) had climbed the Reek (Croagh Patrick) when he visited Mayo, we'd have won these games. Soccer and Fine Gael the main concerns in rural Ireland instead of Fianna Fáil and Gaelic football? The face of Ireland west is surely changing!

Reluctantly I resist her offer 'to come in for a cuppa' and am pleased that the rain clears as I follow her directions to the right of a house and then head uphill. The trail now traverses fields and crosses another minor road before reaching the R330, Wesport/Partry road at Hazel Rock.

Now the trail meanders onwards through a storybook landscape filled with ancient ritualistic sites that are sometimes swallowed by luxuriant vegetation. Here, it seems every wood, lane, Mass rock and holy well comes with a compelling saga. Reputedly, the jewels of Connacht are secreted nearby in caves beneath the cliffs of Aille, but I don't go in search of material riches for it is already afternoon and I need to keep pushing on. The surface is unstable here with several examples of the land collapsing into subterranean river caves. Crossing another road, the path traverses the viewing point of Cloondachon Hill before joining a public road and going left to descend easily into picturesque Aghagower, which contains a medieval church and tenth-century round tower for exploration. What seems more important right now is, however, the fact that it contains a shop with a pub to the rear, where I enjoy a delicious cup of steaming coffee.

Beyond Aghagower I enjoy commanding views as I descend through fields and then follow a well-preserved part of the Tóchar to join a road. Here, the going changes noticeably for now I am mostly footing it along serene, tree-lined country lanes. On one occasion the route dives off-lane to pass by the Boheh Stone, incongruously sited behind a derelict house. This was once a scene of druidic worship and later was reputed to have been a Mass rock used by St Patrick.

Soon after crossing the N59 Westport/Leenane Road, one last excursion through fields and a crossing of the Owenwee River brings me to a tiny road skirting the striking emptiness of Croagh Patrick's south face soaring above. Here, I expect the route to ascend through a former deer park and then over Crott Mountain to join the modern pilgrim route as is clearly shown on my Ordnance Survey map. Instead, the signs point resolutely west along a road that crosses the Western Way long-distance walking route. When we want to get somewhere on foot the landscape around us immediately expands to its

Waymarker on the Tóchar Phádraig.

true proportions. Now, when I just need a shower, a meal and a bed, the road appears to continue interminably. My knees hurt and I feel a blister coming on. Years of climbing high mountains in many countries never caused a problem with blisters but now I have been humbled by a long-distance walk. What can't be cured must be endured, so I continue trudging onwards while wondering if I've missed the route. Then, just as I despair of ever finding a path upwards, a base for Mayo Mountain Rescue comes into view.

Here, I find a trail that proves tiring and steep after a long day but at least leads upwards, in a series of switch-backs. Feeling like a clapped-out mini-car in Mondello Park, I toil heavenwards, while still not sure if I am following the Tóchar. Eventually, I am much relieved to join the modern pilgrim trail to Croagh Patrick where I briefly wrestle with my conscience and win easily.

Some hardy souls, it seems, like to finish the pilgrim trail by continuing to the summit and a little voice tells me 'go up – this is what a proper pilgrim would do.' But I have been told that the Tóchar ends at Murrisk car park, which proves too much of a temptation.

The imminent onset of darkness is my trump card, and I decide to leave the summit untroubled by my presence, for today at least. With my conscience KO'd on the mountainside behind, I make my weary way towards Murrisk. On the descent, however, I receive one last, nasty shock. I can't help but notice waymarkers for a walking route joining my descent path from the east. It is with the dying of the light over the western ocean that I arrive into the car park with a heavy heart and a sad conclusion. It seems that after all my efforts, I have somehow managed to miss the trail and failed to fully complete the Tóchar Phádraig.

Next morning after my Tóchar walk, it is raining again. I head for Westport. Even in the rain, the town has a genuine heartbeat with the sloping streets offering a palpable sense of place. (In 2012 it was voted Ireland's best town in which to live.) The local tourist office will, I hope, once and for all, sort out my confusion at the end of yesterday's outing. Surely Ireland's best-known and by far most-climbed mountain has been rewarded with a unified and definitive map as a thank-you for its valiant contribution to Irish tourism. But the lady in the tourist office shakes her head as she says 'no, nobody's done a map, even though we get people looking for one all the time.'

There is only one thing for it then. Going outside I pull out my ancient and grievously unsmart mobile phone and dial a man whose footprints are to be found on virtually every stone, bog and meadow in the west of Ireland. Gerry Greensmyth is one of Ireland's most experienced hillwalkers and the first to introduce centre-based walking tourism to Ireland. His company, Croagh Patrick Walking Tours, has introduced thousands of visitors to the west of Ireland.

He answers the phone as he is travelling up from Kerry. I tell him that I walked the Tóchar yesterday, but think I went the wrong way near the end.

'Were you up by the Deerpark wall?' he asks.

'No, I followed the signs along a road under Croagh Patrick.'

'Did you see a base for Mayo Mountain Rescue?'

'I did, Gerry.'

'You're all right so. You see, the route of the Tóchar used to go up through the Deerpark and over Crott Mountain. A few years ago it was changed due to an access problem. Now it follows the road that runs on the south side of Croagh Patrick and then up over the coll – so you finished the Tóchar all right.'

'That's great to know, Gerry, but what about the trail I noticed on the way down? It came in just above Murrisk.'

'Ah, don't worry about that. It's the Croagh Patrick Heritage Trail coming all the way from Balla. Trails like these can't go above 300m so they headed it straight for Murrisk.'

Ah, so there are two long-distance trails to Croagh Patrick! I could now safely wear the T-shirt for I had, after all, completed the ancient Tóchar Phádraig from Ballintubber Abbey to Croagh Patrick.

6

CROAGH PATRICK | County Mayo

OVERVIEW Despite the inroads of mass tourism, Croagh Patrick has somehow retained its penitential atmosphere. The route as described offers an opportunity for a fine outing combining parts of three renowned pilgrim trails – the Tóchar Phádraig, the Croagh Patrick Heritage Trail, and the modern Pilgrim Trail – while offering little in the way of navigational difficulties. On a clear day, Croagh Patrick's summit offers a 360-degree view over Clew Bay and of the Connemara and Mayo Mountains.

SUITABILITY This route initially takes the main pilgrim path running from Murrisk to the summit, which is a 7km round trip. Be warned: the final approach to the top is particularly difficult with much loose shale and a gradient rising at 40 degrees. On the descent, you will probably find that two telescopic walking poles are superior to the traditional hazel stick as they are lighter to carry and can be used alternately for support on the steepest part of the path. Afterwards, it is possible either to descend directly along the modern pilgrim path or to follow the much less crowded and more compelling three-pilgrim-route circuit.

GETTING THERE From Westport, follow the R335 west. Immediately beyond Campbell's pub, park in Murrisk car park, located beside the main Louisburg road. The walk starts and finishes here (L919 823).

TIME Allow 4.5 to 5 hours for the full three-trails walk. About 3 to 3.5 hours should be allocated for an up-and-down trip to Croagh Patrick using the modern Pilgrim route.

DISTANCE 7km.

HIGHEST ALTITUDE Croagh Patrick summit 764m.

MAP It presently takes four OSi maps to cover Croagh Patrick fully. However, sheets 30 and 31 are sufficient for the described route.

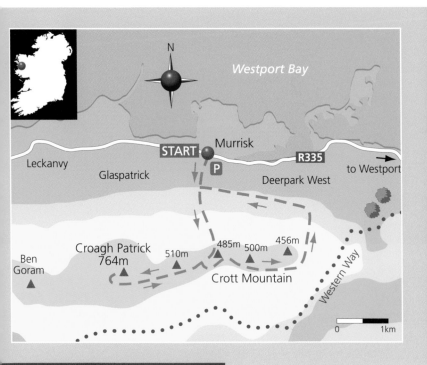

Croagh Patrick

F ive-star walks are two a cent in the Mayo countryside with the Nephin Mountains offering a wonderful escape into one of Ireland's last great wilderness areas. To the south, Mweelrea also presents a beguiling landscape and a memorable mountain challenge, while the Sheeffry Hills remain one of Mayo's best-kept secrets, with isolated grandeur and a strong likelihood that you won't encounter another soul.

By comparison, Croagh Patrick can seem too eroded and overpopulated to satisfy the purist hillwalker. This is particularly true on the last Sunday of July each year when it achieves international renown.

A reflection of Croagh Patrick from Murrisk. (Gareth McCormack)

Then teeming multitudes — many of whom otherwise would never have recourse to a hillside — come in a human avalanche to search for redemption on a tough ascent to the crest of Ireland's quintessential holy mountain. And this may also be the reason why, year round, hillwalkers tend to give Croagh Patrick a wide berth perhaps, reckoning the continually busy and heavily eroded pilgrim highway leading from Murrisk to the summit suits masochists more than mountaineers.

Another explanation may be that while the modern pilgrim route to Croagh Patrick's summit is relatively straightforward from a navigation point of view, the remainder of the mountain can be rather confusing with no fewer than four Ordnance Survey maps required to cover the area in its entirety. Yet, despite these drawbacks, I find it quite impossible to visit Westport without being drawn to the ancient pilgrim route on Ireland's holiest summit.

And now I am intrigued by the apparent medley of trails around Croagh Patrick. So to plan my next move and escape the rain, I head for a coffee in the Chilli Café on Main Street. Immediately it seems I'm back in the 1980s and in college again. A middle-aged man with a mid-

Atlantic accent is perched on a high stool in lecturer pose with a puddle of wet-looking British students seated around a large table below him. He appears to know all there is to be known about the west of Ireland, from Creevykeel to Carrowmore to Carraroe, but he particularly wants the group to visit some caves near Cong. 'They're really interesting caves,' he enthuses, 'ideal for a day like this'. When I was there, I didn't go very far down because I didn't have a torch, but if you have lights, you can go really far.

As I leave the café the rain eases as if to reinforce the saying, 'rain at seven, clear by eleven'. Soon I find myself loitering in the well-appointed visitor centre lying beside the trailhead for the modern pilgrim trail from Murrisk. Here, a group of overseas visitors is preparing for its Croagh Patrick ascent by hiring the hazel sticks which for generations have been the pilgrim's traditional friend, even though telescopic walking poles are lighter and more practical these days. Finally, when the last of the rain takes itself off in the direction of Castlebar, I set out by retracing

View over Clew Bay from Croagh Patrick's pilgrim track.

A barefoot pilgrim descends Croagh Patrick. (Valerie O'Sullivan)

my footsteps of yesterday. Initially my feet ache badly as a result of the previous day's exertions as I toil slowly up the boot-battered trail, past a statue of Ireland's national apostle.

Arriving at the saddle where the main track leads right for the summit, I find that the ache in my feet is now just a dull twinge. Here, it occurs to me that the wonderful thing about Croagh Patrick is not only how it commemorates mankind's seemingly timeless attraction to high places, but also celebrates the colourful mosaic of human life. Accompanying me is a eclectic mishmash of hazel-stick pilgrims, barefooted penitents, well-kitted ramblers, inscrutable peak baggers, insouciant Europeans and even a couple of fell runners with alarmingly snazzy tops and ruthlessly chiselled bodies. And, finally, there's a group of lightly clad Irish youths displaying a valiant indifference to the chilling breeze while carrying plastic bags that clank suspiciously like cans.

Continuing to trudge upwards, I follow an unruly spider's web of intermingling paths over shockingly bad screes. Stopping for a moment, I can't help but marvel at the way mountains such as Croagh Patrick peel away the cares and trappings of civilisation and force us to concentrate exclusively on the task in hand. Everyone is resolutely in the moment here and while some are wafting upwards as if propelled by the summer breeze, others are struggling badly. Nearby a man whose face has turned an alarming lobster red is clearly losing the battle with gravity. He is reduced to stumbling and crawling but he persists to the summit. Here, he just manages to cross himself once before subsiding into a sweating heap.

Others are arriving with enough energy left to take in their surroundings. I sense a little disenchantment as these first-timers glance around the nondescript summit plateau. I wonder if they were half-expecting greater things – to be greeted by an ethereal vision of a mountain Madonna or to encounter an undernourished St Patrick, struggling to lock his GPS on an errant heavenly satellite. It's hard to be sure what they expect but there is no denying that a couple of thousand years of pilgrimage has left its mark on the summit. Immediately obvious is the relatively modern and not strikingly attractive chapel sitting rather incongruously on its rocky throne. Then there are also rudimentary toilets, more penitential stations and several untidy shelters.

The beauty of Croagh Patrick is not in the immediate, however, but in the distant. On a clear day, pilgrims can view a landscape little altered since St Patrick reputedly trod these selfsame stones. Today is one of these, and so it is possible to savour views of the great sweep over multi-islanded Clew Bay to the great wildness of Mayo's mountains and moorlands. Few clichés remain unhackneyed in describing this panorama so rather then risk adding another, let's just say it competes strongly for the title of Ireland's finest vista.

Holy mountains are supposed to be contemplative places and now I sit back and try to understand what it is that has drawn so many believers over the generations. Is it the enigmatic quality of this mountain – its striking prominence and reassuring permanence in contrast to our own transience and triviality? Avarice may now squat immovably at the core of modern life but the undiminished appeal of Croagh Patrick is incontrovertible proof of some unquenchable human desire for higher meaning beyond the meaninglessness of conspicuous consumption.

Then for a few moments, all heaven breaks loose. A mostly female group of American college students pile noisily onto the summit and celebrate the achievement with an extravagant rejoicing more appropriate, one might imagine, for the pinnacle of Everest. There are hugs, kisses, and high-fives all round and even a couple of self-conscious-looking Irish lads are drawn into the uninhibited celebrations. Having long held the belief that a man should embrace every female opportunity that life presents, I hang around expectantly but am rewarded only with a half-hearted high-five from a burly guy who, I guess, is probably the college quarterback.

Next, I notice the now-no-longer-lobster-faced man has recovered and is nonchalantly reciting a rosary beside one of the summit prayer beds. I begin descending the unpleasant screes which remind me, as they always do, of walking downhill on a river of ball bearings. Here the track is clearly succumbing to the enormous footfall and great care must be exercised since this is the prime accident black spot on the Reek. When I reach yet another penitential station, however, it is possible to breathe a sigh of relief for the slope eases as the route meanders east.

Here, I stop to gaze south over the Mayo outback to the Sheeffry Hills and the spikey Connemara Mountains protruding beyond, with the route of the Tóchar now clearly visible as it ascends towards me. I have just concluded that these are indeed fertile lands for myth-making when a question comes from behind which jolts me back to the twenty-first century. 'Hey, mister! Is it far to the top?' Believing the old adage that one should be suspicious of those calling you 'mister' at a first encounter, I turn around and am confronted by an entire family on the move. There is a woman wearing a yellow top, leggings and kitten heels and a couple of teenage girls dressed as if they are heading for a post-exam party. But it is the man who most catches my attention for, oblivious to the dangers, he has seated high on his shoulders a whimpering lad who can't be much more than two. They're genuine pilgrims, though, carrying a small statue of the Blessed Virgin, and when I tell them it's less then an hour to the top, it seems to please them.

Now hillwalking is, of course, all about self-reliance and I also believe that life is easier if you don't make enemies by accident. Still, this situation seems to require some kind of intervention. 'I don't know if you will be able to carry that young man to the summit – it gets quite steep, you know, and it's very tricky coming down. Maybe one of you should stay here with him while the rest go on.'

'Ah, not at all,' says the woman, 'he'll be fine. He just gets like this sometimes.'

With a final 'will ye get goin', the woman turns and frogmarches the teenagers up the mountain, closely followed by the man, with the young lad still wobbling precariously a couple of metres above the rocks.

I have other things to think about, however, for the modern path swings left from the saddle and continues downwards from here. Generally, I dislike retracing my steps and Gerry Greensmyth had whetted my appetite about the Croagh Patrick Heritage Trail. Suddenly, I decide, it's time to lose the modern path and reclaim some solitude.

Striking out east I pick up a less distinct trail running on the south side of hydra-headed Crott Mountain. This is the original route of the Tóchar Phádraig that Gerry Greensmyth spoke about. Now entirely alone, I find myself traversing beside a large tumbled-down drystone wall that was originally built to keep deer from straying. Crossing and recrossing this wall several times, I eventually descend steeply to intersect a waymarked route.

Here, I encounter the aforementioned Croagh Patrick Heritage Trail. Later I discover that this is 61km long – considerably longer than the distance I walked from Ballintubber – and comprises a variety of underfoot conditions including road, farmland, forest paths and bog roads.

Now following the reassuring waymarkers of the Heritage Trail, I continue north and downhill until the arrows swing abruptly left to parallel the Louisburg road. Completing this final section back to Murrisk, I conclude that, while Croagh Patrick may indeed be too busy and scarred by generations of penitents to satisfy the purist hillwalker, this is really of little consequence. What matters here is the long tradition of the redemptive journey that continues strongly to this day as enduring proof of the restless human search for intangible values that materialism inevitably leaves unsatisfied.

7

MAUMEEN | County Galway

OVERVIEW A pleasant and relatively quiet pilgrim trail with many echoes from Ireland's Christian past at the head of the pass. Those wishing to shorten the walk can leave a car in a small car park above Cur, L926 523, near the end of the north-east track from Maumeen.

SUITABILITY Unchallenging outing on well-defined tracks and quiet back roads with the greatest danger being the unlikely possibility of being run over by a tractor. For the full traverse of Maumeen it is best to leave a second car at Keane's Pub, Maum. Otherwise, you will need a friend or a taxi to bring you back to your start point in the Inagh Valley.

GETTING THERE From Galway, take the N59 for Clifden. Be sure to follow the signs west through Maam Cross for Clifden. Beyond Maam Cross, go right at L872 475 and follow the *Slí Chonamara* signs for about 3km to reach Maumeen car park which is located on the right-hand side of the road (L891 495). *Note: the* Slí Chonamara *is not marked on the OSi maps.*

TIME About 3.5 hours.

DISTANCE 9km.

MAP OSi *Discovery Series* 37, 38, and 44 cover the route in its entirety. Stay on the track, however, and you shouldn't need a map.

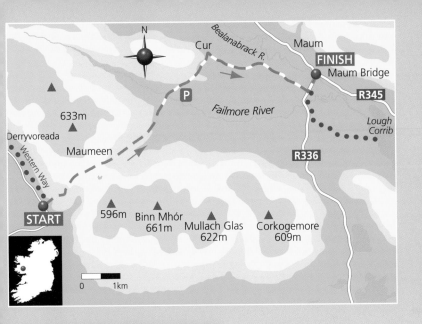

Maumeen

It is amazing how much we miss when we're in a hurry. I had been down the sensational road south from Louisburg to Connemara before, but always journeying with an objective in mind, perhaps Galway, maybe Clifden. This time, however, I dawdle my way south from Westport, for my goal is nearby. And my leisurely pace immediately allows the majestic three-dimensional complexities and changing colours of Ireland's west to unfold as never before.

This is undoubtedly one of Ireland's finest and captivating road journeys, surrounded by some of the wildest and most spectacular mountains anywhere. But there is another side to its imposing setting. Beside the road, I pause briefly at a monument commemorating one of the saddest events of the Irish Potato Famine.

In 1849, a group of about 150 people, who lived in aching poverty, set out from Louisbourg on what amounted to a desperate pilgrimage. They didn't travel in search of spiritual nourishment, though, but instead to intercede for physical sustenance in the form of food, for many were in the process of starving to death. At Delphi, the famine commissioners, who were responsible for giving famine relief, were apparently having lunch and refused help. The group were then forced to struggle back to Louisburg through a snowstorm with many dying en route.

Looking west from Maumeen over Connemara.

And, of course, here we have the dilemma of scenery – it's magnificent and inspirational, but only on a full stomach. The vistas we consider sublime and arresting today must have seemed repugnant, threatening and even hellish to these starving people. Beauty to their eyes would, I guess, not have been stark, unproductive mountains. Their Promised Land would surely have been flat, boring, dry lowland that could have provided plentiful sustenance to ensure their survival.

Tired of driving and reminded by growing hunger pangs that you can't survive on scenery alone, I pull in at an atmospheric-looking roadside pub. The sign says 'food served all day', and I briefly mull over my good fortune to live in a time and part of the world where food is available in abundance. There is no one in the bar and the place seems spookily empty. Eventually, a waiter appears and hands me a menu with a flourish. I ask about the soup of the day and he vanishes to check. Soon he is back with an answer. 'It's Daniel O'Donnell soup today,' he tells me cheerily. Since Daniel O'Donnell is a hugely popular Donegal-born singer, I have visions of some exotic concoction: perhaps Donegal Bay prawns, Lough Swilly oysters and Tory

Island turnips. So I am slightly disappointed when vegetable soup arrives. However, it is rich and smooth and very satisfying.

After lunch, heading on down the magnificent Inagh Valley, I swing left towards Derryvoreada with the dramatic scenery still refusing to relent. Eventually, at a small parking place, I pull in and follow the signs uphill for Maumeen ('the pass of the birds'). St Patrick reputedly chanced this way in the fifth century but observing the Godforsaken, watery expanse of south Connemara he, understandably perhaps, refused to go further. He did, however, create a strong pilgrim tradition, without the inconvenience of getting his sandals wet, by blessing Connemara from where he stood.

As I ascend the stony trail, I notice that there are few reminders of past spiritual resonances. I had visited Maumeen from a different direction about twenty years ago in such abysmal weather conditions that I hardly noticed the place. I was with a group taking on the Maumturks Challenge – a long-distance walk covering 25km over the toughest, most unforgiving Connemara terrain with a total ascent of over 2,300m included. It is generally regarded as the hardest challenge walk in Ireland and we certainly didn't disbelieve this at the end of the day when we gratefully slithered to the finish in Leenaun after a 10-hour drenching on the mountainsides.

Oratory at Maumeen.

Today, the weather is resolutely benign and when I come to the head of the pass it is immediately obvious that Maumeen remains an important pilgrim site. There are all the usual trappings of pilgrimage: an oratory, an outdoor altar, a rocky cleft where St Patrick reputedly slept, a statue of the saint and Stations of the Cross.

Apparently, Maumeen was originally a prehistoric location for druidic worship that, like many others, was Christianised. However, with the suppression of Catholicism in the seventeenth and eighteenth centuries, the annual pattern day celebration in early August became somewhat secular. Connemara folk came up from the south-west, as I had just done, while people from the Joyce Country ascended from Maum. Almost inevitably drunkenness and faction fighting took over. The result was that the penitential tradition almost died away but was revived in 1980 by Fr McGreil, a local priest. These days it has proudly risen again as an important destination with major organised pilgrimages on St Patrick's Day, Good Friday and on an August Sunday.

There are already scatterings of walkers and overseas visitors pottering around the site when I arrive but none seems to have a spiritual motive for their visit. The site clearly has an ongoing spiritual dimension, however, for a nearby holy well honouring St Patrick is laden with small offerings to the Almighty and a couple of poignant Mass cards dedicated to loved ones lost.

Lingering awhile in the pleasant sunshine, I can't help wondering at the ubiquity of Patrician mythology across Ireland. How did Patrick and the others who introduced Christianity to Ireland manage to weave such an inescapable spiritual net that it immediately ensnared the entire population of Ireland, when later attempts by a succession of English monarchs to introduce Protestantism met with fierce resistance and ultimately proved a failure? Clearly, after his long sojourn in Ireland Patrick, would – unlike later Protestant evangelisers – have enjoyed the considerable advantage of familiarity with the Irish language. But could it also be that the promise of eternal happiness in the afterlife was the unique selling point, elevating the new religion above its predecessor? Or did Patrick and his fellow missionaries succeed by cleverly overlaying new beliefs upon existing rites and rituals while English monarchs made the mistake of dissolving monasteries and persecuting priests in the attempt to impose an entirely new religious order?

With scant information available, it is clearly almost impossible, even for those far more knowledgeable than I, to capture the reality of the monumental social shift that occurred in Ireland in the fifth century. Whatever the reason for the success of the Christian mission to Ireland, it unerringly propelled Patrick to world superstar status on each successive 17 March.

I could now retrace my steps upwards from the Inagh Valley, but as a hopeless new experiences addict, I descend instead the north-east side of the pass. This proves a captivating excursion with the time-warp beauty of the majestic Maum Valley and the Joyce Country hills beckoning beyond. Passing through a couple of gates I eventually fetch up on a quiet road. Continuing about 5km, while enjoying friendly waves from cheery locals, I reach the Galway–Leenane road and, soon after, Keane's hostelry in the village of Maum. My day ends with hot toddies by the fireside, while waiting, not too impatiently I must admit, for the arrival of my prearranged lift back to the Inagh Valley.

8

CLONMACNOISE
PILGRIM CYCLE | County Offaly

OVERVIEW A pleasant enough outing with the most interesting scenery coming along the spine of the Esker Riada near the end. Probably too short to attract committed cyclists or genuine pilgrims though. A pleasant alternative to the cycle would be to walk the Esker Riada from Mannion's Cross Roads to Clonmacnoise.

For those not wishing to cycle, the most atmospheric way of getting to Clonmacnoise is the way the founder must surely have intended. In summer there are sailings from picturesque Shannonbridge to the serene landing place beside what was once the beating heart of Irish monasticism. Along the way the boat passes through the ecologically significant Shannon Callows, which in summer boast a profusion of wild flowers that offer a refuge to the corncrake, now one of Ireland's most endangered bird species.

SUITABILITY The terrain on the Pilgrim Cycle route to Clonmacnoise contains nothing to challenge even the most uncommitted leisure cyclist.

GETTING THERE The cycle begins from the shrine in the centre of Ballycumber village (N620 730), County Offaly, on the R436 between Clara and Ferbane.

FINISH The early Christian monastery at Clonmacnoise (N009 306). To return to Ballycumber, cyclists will need either to organise a lift from Clonmacnoise or cycle back. .

TIME Anywhere between 1 and 2 hours depending on cycling experience.

DISTANCE 22km.   **MAP** OSi *Discovery Series* 47 and 48.

Morning mist over Temple Finghin and the River Shannon,
Clonmacnoise. (Gareth McCormack)

Enticing as it is to blame the growth of rampart materialism in Irish society for the century-long decline in the strong nineteenth-century pilgrimage tradition of footing it to a sacred destination, the real culprit is almost certainly the automobile. In the early years, we can assume, penitents mostly followed the line of least resistance to their destinations. Why should they do otherwise? Pilgrims sought, after all, not fitness, flat tummies or sublime scenery but spiritual renewal. Common sense would, therefore, suggest they pursued the most recognised routes to their objectives. These rights of way eventually became modern roads, many of which then became speedy highways to accommodate the seemingly insatiable twentieth-century demands of the motor car. Boot-burning bitumen is not at all welcoming to walkers, though, and it is unsurprising that fewer pilgrims cared to ramble along hard shoulders with endless lines of traffic thundering past.

Solutions have been found with some of Ireland's most popular trails being diverted away from their original medieval highways to quieter country roads and lanes. On parts of the Spanish Camino, separate

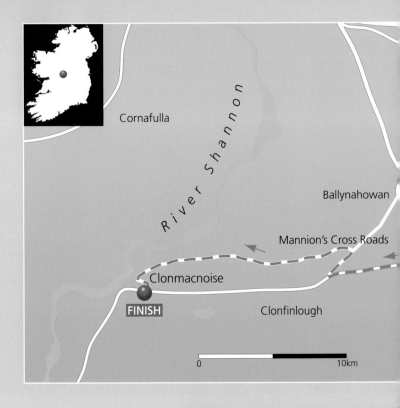

walking routes have been placed beside but shielded from the main highways. And in the case of what were once one of Ireland's busiest ancient highways, the solution has been found in the innovative form of a cycle trail.

Those who made the huge effort, during the early Irish Christian period, to journey from the European mainland to the great powerhouse of learning at Clonmacnoise were, for the most part, not pilgrims, but those in search of scholarship. Those were days when Ireland had a well-deserved reputation as a 'land of saints and scholars' and while much of Europe wallowed in the Dark Ages, erudition, artistic endeavour and piety found a safe place to flourish within the monasteries of Ireland.

These early knowledge seekers walked from abbey to abbey, and the abbey at Leamonaghan near what is now the Offaly village of Ballycumber was usually their last stop, as it was conveniently located an easy walk

from Clonmacnoise. From here, their final outing was along the crest of the Esker Riada ridge, which afforded dry underfoot conditions and absorbing views over the surrounding countryside.

Initially, the idea of a cycling trail seemed oddly incongruous for what is billed a pilgrim route. But pilgrimage traditionally involves any form of non-mechanised transport and it is common, these days, to encounter cyclists as well as horseback riders on the devotional trails of Europe.

As far as I'm concerned, off-road cycling is fine, but sharing tarmac in a game of chicken with cars, trucks and silage harvesters is an entirely different kettle of scary fish. Then there is the fact that the Offaly flatlands are more noted for beef and peat than stunning scenery. And finally, there is the not inconsiderable problem of finding a suitable conveyance. To this end I head out to the garden shed and excavate a decade's accumulation of rubbish to try and locate my ancient mountain bike. It emerges battered, bruised and totally unusable. Clearly, this sad pile of twisting, rusting neglect isn't taking me anywhere.

It seems the glorious cycling revolution of the past few years has somehow passed me by. Then a faint memory stirs of the Green Party's 'Bike to Work' scheme and the flashy new ladies' high Nellie that had appeared outside my front door soon afterwards, courtesy of my wife. But where is it now? On a hunch I head for the other shed and there, skulking unloved behind disused carpets and old furniture, is the answer to my pilgrim prayer – an as-new, three-speed ladies' roadster complete with wicker basket. Outside, I hop on and wobble uncertainly around the tarmac a few times. The handlebars are a bit too high, the saddle far too low, but pilgrims can't be choosers, so this will have to be my steed for the Clonmacnoise Pilgrim Trail.

A few days later, I find myself standing with some trepidation beside a shrine to a saint I had previously never heard of in a sleepy little Offaly village I have also never heard of. St Manchan is apparently Ballycumber's representative in heavenly places and has been rewarded for this with an ornate statue that represents the start point for my penitential journey.

With my water bottle and rain jacket in the basket, I pedal uncertainly out of Ballycumber. Soon after, I find a huge supermarket truck on my tail, and am glad to escape up a minor road. At a T-junction, the arrows point left. In the absence of any other signage I obey this and very quickly find myself on a main road without directional arrows, so there is no option but to retrace my route.

Back almost in Ballycumber I am poring over an inadequate map with furrowed brow when a local man chances upon the scene. 'Where are you off to,' he asks. When I say Clonmacnoise, he replies, 'that's a quare way you're going all right'. Decently, however, he refrains from commenting on my antiquated mode of transport. Instead he tells me to go right at the T-junction and then left at the next intersection. 'But what about the signs?' 'Ah, don't mind the signs. Just follow these directions and you'll be in Clonmacnoise before you know it.' I set off again and soon after fetch up in the small village of Boherfadda. (See author's note at end of chapter.)

Here I decide to make to make a stop at a twelfth-century shrine to the aforementioned St Manchan, which is apparently made of yew wood and gilded bronze and is considered to be a masterpiece of early Irish Christian art. My guidebook tells me that the shrine is held under the tightest security in the local parish church.

Expectantly, I head inside and poke around unsuccessfully for the shrine. Then a local woman comes in and tells me it is not presently on display, because just a few days prior to my arrival, it had been stolen.

Now hoping that a severely fit, lycra-clad apparition on a carbon fibre machine won't glide easily past with a condescending smile, I pedal gamely onwards. Along the way, I make a quick diversion to examine St Manchan's Holy Well, which is signposted a short distance off the route. The saint obviously has a considerable following locally, for much effort has been expended to secure the surrounds of the well and put a statue of Manchan in the wall above the water.

The Offaly countryside doesn't exactly offer a knockout vista; it's actually a bit like watching the Irish soccer team play – pleasant enough at times, provided you make due allowances and your expectations aren't too high in the first place. Certainly, the midland topography is not compelling in a biscuit-tin pretty sense, but the fertile rolling countryside does possess undoubted charm. And later when I briefly encounter a main road near the village of Doon, it serves to remind me of how traffic free the entire journey has been so far.

It is now time to ascend onto the spine of the famous Esker Riada. My guidebook tells me that this ridge was created by the deposits of sand, gravel and boulders, carried by rivers flowing beneath an ice age glacier. When the glacier melted 10,000 years ago, these deposits remained to form a fertile ridge. And, indeed, my route now rises sublimely above the surrounding bogs, offering extended views over the surrounding countryside. There is here a certain richness to the commonplace Irish countryside that I now find a source of simple pleasure while also reflecting that this elevated view of any approaching danger must have been a comforting source of security for early Christian travellers. A few shortish climbs have me panting a bit, but generally the going is easy and my high-tech three-speed gear copes admirably.

Cross of the Scriptures at Clonmacnoise.

As I begin a slow descent from the Esker, the first couple of trail users I have encountered all day appear ahead, as they foot it dutifully towards Clonmacnoise. Then, as the languid waters of the River Shannon materialise to my right, I become aware that the route has undeniably drawn me in. A round tower appears on the horizon and immediately puts me in mind of the lines from a poem I learned in school. 'In a quiet watered land, a land of roses, stands St Kieran's city fair.' Roses are not very much in evidence, but otherwise the sentiments here seem accurate, for St Kieran's dreamy city is now laid out below, with the sweep of the great river as a surreal backdrop. And somehow it seems I have now exited the dreary cares of the twenty-first century and retuned to the quiet ways and timeless sounds of another more harmonious age. Then it's downhill past the ruins of the Nun's Church, which I later discover is akin to Cormac's Chapel at the Rock of Cashel. One of the best examples of Hiberno-Romanesque architecture in Ireland, it contains an ornate doorway which is considered the finest of its kind in Ireland. Unaware of this, I don't feel an urge to explore and so I head on for Clonmacnoise instead

As I enter the site, it is easy to see how these lush, well-watered lands attracted saints and scholars, plunderers and planters for countless generations. A guide is showing a group of German visitors around, while their group leader translates. He tells them that Clonmacnoise owes its importance as a great monastic city to the fact that it was founded by St Kieran at what was then the crossroads of Ireland. The saint did not survive long, but he had already planted the seed corn for a great city. Buildings were mostly of wood in the early years and once covered 10 acres, he informs them. Later, many of these were replaced with stone structures including a cathedral, seven churches, two round towers, three high crosses and a large number of early Christian gravestones. The group is enraptured by it all, but even when the guide moves to describing the superb Cross of the Scriptures, I find that I'm not in the mood for it. I drift away and am drawn through a small gate towards the lazy meander of the River Shannon.

By the riverbank I sit and absorb the hypnotic stillness. There is a deep serenity to the place, as swans glide imperiously by in dancing river light; an impertinent moorhen suddenly breaks the silence, while ripples spread where fish rise languorously. And nearby, I notice a group of visitors for Clonmacnoise are disembarking from a boat, having arrived via Ireland's greatest waterway.

Little changed since ancient times, the River Shannon remains almost exactly as St Kieran might have seen it. And it is then the thought comes to me that the true glory of Clonmacnoise, which raises it head and shoulders above other monastic sites from the same period, arises from its sublime location beside the Shannon. Cycling to Clonmanoise has its moments, but river-borne travel is surely the true way to reconnect with the journey of scholarly pilgrims past to this once renowned European seat of Christian learning.

Author's note: I mentioned above some difficulty with signposting when completing the above route on my original 2012 pilgrim journey. On my return to complete the route in 2016, the signage was immeasurably improved. No junction was without one or sometimes two directional arrows, while for much of the route even townlands were signposted. Clonmacnoise Pilgrim Road now qualifies as the most comprehensively signposted pilgrim trail in Ireland.

9

ST KEVIN'S WAY | County Wicklow

Hollywood to Glendalough

OVERVIEW The pilgrim trail from Hollywood to Glendalough in County Wicklow follows well-marked tracks that rise gently to the Wicklow Gap and then descends benignly to the finish at the ancient monastic ruins. Those who abominate road walking might be well served by starting their walk from Ballinagee Bridge, which is located on the R756. From this point, the amount of road walking is reduced to a minimum and all the most scenic parts of the route still lie ahead. As this is a linear route, you will need a car pre-placed at the finish in Glendalough. Otherwise a friend or a taxi is required to collect you and drop you back to your start point in Hollywood.

SUITABILITY Generally presents no objective dangers or navigational difficulties except the problem of sharing narrow, footpath-less roads with speeding cars. Walkers should, as always, have boots and warm clothing and, of course, rainwear.

GETTING THERE Take the N81 from Dublin or the R411 from Naas through Ballymore Eustace to the small Wicklow village of Hollywood. The trailhead for St Kevin's Way is close by the village centre (N939 054).

FINISH The ancient Christian monastery at Glendalough (T120 969).

TIME At least 6 hours.

DISTANCE 30km.

HIGHEST ALTITUDE Wicklow Gap, 460m.

MAP OSi *Discovery Series 56.*

St Kevin's Way.

haven't walked very much in County Wicklow. The gentle whaleback nature of the mountains does not draw me as strongly as the beckoning bleakness of the untamed Kerry and Connemara Mountains. And somewhere deep in the landscape of my subconscious, it seems, I hold a belief that a true pilgrim route should terminate somewhere near Ireland's western seaboard. I don't know why this should be but, nevertheless, it seems just a little strange to be heading east rather than west on a summer morning to follow in what are billed 'the footsteps of St Kevin' in County Wicklow. My guidebook informs me St Kevin first lived in a monastery at Kilnamanagh, which lies outside present-day Dublin. Later he moved on to the wild fastness of Glendalough in search of seclusion for uninterrupted prayer and mortification of the flesh, but this wish for solitude paradoxically attracted large numbers of followers to his place of escape and a monastery was thus founded. After Kevin's death in 618, Glendalough developed into an impressive monastic city, which continued as a centre of piety and learning that rivalled Clonmacnoise. The torch of learning burned brightly here for many centuries, with medieval pilgrims coming from far and wide, not only to visit Kevin's tomb, but also to imbibe of cutting-edge scholarship. Further encouragement came their way when the pope promulgated a kind of medieval '7 for 1 special offer'. He obligingly declared that seven visits to Glendalough would equal one to Rome in terms of indulgences gained.

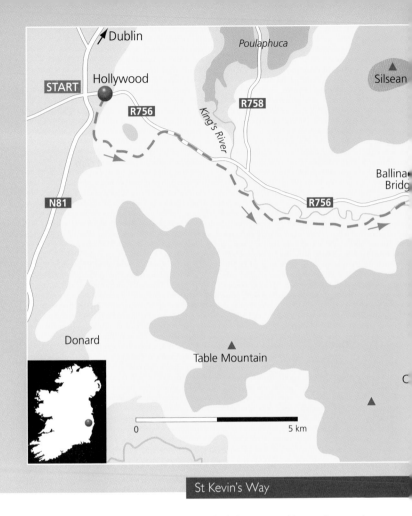

And indeed my search for easy indulgences, without the modern redemptive exercise of passing through busy airports, begins promisingly enough from the quiet olde-worlde charm of Hollywood village. From here, St Kevin's Way follows a picturesque glen, passing an abandoned quarry, a statue of the saint and the cave where he reputedly slept as he made his way to Glendalough. This makes me wonder what is it with saints and caves. Why was it almost a prerequisite for early Christian sainthood to have taken up residence in a cave at least once?

Beyond the glen, things go steeply downhill. After a short walk on a public road I turn up left onto a laneway and a long uphill climb for about 1.5km. This part of the route should only be completed, I guess, as part of

a genuine effort of atonement for grievous sins or by those condemned to write guidebooks.

The narrow road is surrounded by relentlessly high banks and no footpaths. So when I encounter a car I am forced to scramble up these banks. Suddenly contemplating the unfortunate consequences of meeting a milk truck or something bigger, I pant ahead hurriedly to escape this claustrophobic lane, while concluding that, heavy vehicles aside, it stretches credulity to believe that this would have been the path chosen by early penitents heading for Glendalough. Fortunately, there isn't any further traffic and eventually the route concedes to a somewhat wider road at a point offering splendid views south over Hollywood Glen to

Church Mountain. The huge summit cairn atop this eminence contains the remains of the eponymous church that was an important pilgrimage site up to the eighteenth century. A more benign road now leads me directly back to the main R756. To my consternation, I now discover I am still only about 2km outside Hollywood.

There seems no help for it but to trudge on with traffic whizzing past and no hard margin to provide a modicum of safety. After a couple of kilometres I escape, with a sigh of relief, onto a sinuous minor road leading right. Conscious that so far St Kevin's Way has proven something of a disappointment, I follow this seemingly interminable byroad, which I can't help noticing offers little in the way of reminders that it genuinely traces the footsteps of an early Christian saint. Instead, huge dispiriting electricity pylons, that really should have been placed underground, march northwest through the valley from the hydroelectricity generation station at Turlough Hill.

My attitude to the route is not improved when it begins raining heavily just as the tarmac ends abruptly in a farmyard. Here, I flap around in a cold, penetrating downpour while concluding morosely that writing books about trail walking is indeed a wretched business. I poke around in the rain and eventually discover the trail continuing through a field before entering a dripping forest. Beyond the trees, the route veers left to reach the banks of the King's River. The going is pleasant enough along the riverbank as the downpour eases to a drizzle.

Next, the waymarkers take me across a concrete bridge over the King's River and along a forest road to rejoin the R756. Here, St Kevin's Way doubles back a little confusingly towards Hollywood, before joining

Round tower at Glendalough.
(Paula Elmore)

at Ballinagee Bridge with the pilgrim path coming in from Valleymount.

Now the fun begins: the trail plays hide-and-seek with the main road as it ascends to the walk's highest elevation at the Wicklow Gap by diving abruptly in and out of what are mostly unremarkable stands of commercial timber. First, it enters woodlands on the north side of the road and follows a forest roadway for about a 100m until the waymarkers convey me right and uphill along an enclosed greenway. Then the forest suddenly parts to reveal the ancient field system surrounding a strangely poignant farmstead.

Crossing the fields behind the abandoned farmhouse makes for a pleasant diversion from forestry and has me wondering, when did this place last ring to children's laughter and what became of the people who once called this place home. The thought is soon behind me, as I tag a forest firebreak and then continue through some mixed woodland to regain the R756 after about a kilometre. Immediately it departs the highway on the south side this time. Here the going is agreeable, if unspectacular, as the path periodically enters and emerges from dense forestry while also crossing a couple of pretty wooden footbridges. Then I am glad to discover a narrow boardwalk has been added in places to assist my crossing some of the boggier sections Soon after, I find myself paralleling the R756 for a time before conceding to the tarmac just short of the Wicklow Gap as the sun finally explodes forth from behind the clouds.

Ireland's Garden County has, in recent years, become a weekend retreat for city dwellers seeking a cure for 'nature deficit disorder'. Today the gap is buzzing with recreationalists – walkers, cyclists, Harley Davidson riders and day trippers all absorbing the sublime views. Immediately captivated by the stroll-stopping vistas, I am forced to concede to having somehow grossly underestimated the beauty of Wicklow. The vista from the Gap, across sweeping mountain and moorland, rivals the best to be found further west and immediately reminds me how lucky Dubliners are to have such an immense outdoor amenity on their doorstep.

I now feel my mood lift, as the nature of the terrain changes dramatically with open mountainside replacing forestry and bright sunshine replacing overcast skies. The pleasant trail now rambles downhill before crossing the road to Lough Nahanagan and then skirting a forest. Here I am definitely in the footsteps of the saints for the ancient flagstones of the old pilgrim path are still visible, providing a physical link to the route's early Christian past. Beyond the forest, the path takes me over a stile to join a gravel track leading across a stream to rejoin the main R756.

This final road excursion is mercifully short, however, and then it is again off-road, on the right, at a scenic bridge. Now, I begin a spectacular descent into Glendasan, while soothed by the musical accompaniment of hurrying water. There are some ruined dwellings along the way that clearly represent the now forgotten dreams of families past who tried and ultimately failed to make a life in this unforgiving landscape. Here it occurs to me, and not for the first time, how the buildings of past generations seem to fit into the landscape with effortless grace, while their modern-day counterparts are so often intrusively unblending.

Next I come across the remains of a once thriving lead mine. Lead extraction in the area eventually fell victim to the notorious boom-to-bust cycle of the mining industry, but at the time of the Irish Potato Famine was crucially important to the economy of Wicklow. During the worst of the Great Hunger, these mines ensured the survival of many, with employment for 200 men who produced over 100 tons of lead ore monthly.

Beyond the mine workings, the path follows the south bank of the Glendasan River on a well-laid gravel track leading past a couple of retreat houses. Now, I head on by the riverside along a compellingly enclosed sylvan trail and enter the haunting and secluded valley where Saint Kevin spent his life in prayer and contemplation.

Today, it doesn't feel very secluded, for Glendalough is now one of the most important cards up the sleeve of Irish tourism and seems to groan under the weight of visitors. As I walk the short distance to enter the ancient monastic site, a traffic snarl-up has developed, caused by two touring coaches outside the Glendalough Hotel and there are people everywhere. There are cyclists, joggers, walkers, tour groups, day trippers and a group of retail therapy seekers browsing the outdoor stalls.

Just inside the ornate entrance to the monastic ruins an ebullient-looking bride and shell-shocked groom are having their photograph taken, accompanied by a typically huge Irish wedding party. Further on, a guide is telling a group of young Americans that little now remains of the early monastery that established itself around Kevin's tomb, and most of the surviving buildings date from the eleventh and twelfth centuries, including one of Ireland's best preserved examples of a round tower. Then he dispatches them to walk to the Upper Lake and I follow in their footsteps as we wander serenely along gentle, aromatic paths.

Soon, I am beside the Upper Lake, drinking in the tranquil beauty of the tightly enclosed valley laid out before me. I fell for Glendalough on my first visit over three decades ago and now I can see how this happened. The valley before me exudes a deeply mysterious and hauntingly alluring quality that is difficult to quantify but which unmistakably denotes it as a place apart. Gazing across the still waters it occurs to me that the attraction of Ireland West lies with the austere, forbidding and untamable mountain extravaganza. The beauty of Glendalough is, however, on a simpler, less awesome scale. Here is a truly intimate grandeur where people are gently absorbed by a landscape possessing near perfect harmony, as if created by the hand of an all-powerful heavenly architect.

10

ST KEVIN'S WAY | County Wicklow

Valleymount to Ballinagee Bridge

OVERVIEW Surprisingly little is lost by the fact that the Valleymount Pilgrim Spur almost entirely follows public roads. The linear nature of the route and the fact that these roads are little frequented and highly scenic makes for an unexpectedly contemplative and rewarding outing.

SUITABILITY Unchallenging walk almost entirely following quiet country roads. Height gain of 120m.

GETTING THERE From Blessington, County Wicklow, take the N81 south towards Hollywood. Leave the N81 by following the R758 left. Cross two bridges and continue to your start point, which is outside St Joseph's Catholic Church, Valleymount. (N921 076).

TIME 2 hours.   **DISTANCE** 8km.

MAP OSi *Discovery Series* 56.

I had never been to the west Wicklow village of Valleymount, but the name had, nonetheless, seeped into my consciousness. Akin to Little Bighorn, USA, and Dry River, New Zealand, the village's appellation struck me as a classic oxymoron. This idiosyncrasy didn't particularly make me want to rush off there, however. Then I looked it up on the map and couldn't wait to visit, for what immediately leaped at me was the fact that it appeared to enjoy the most sublime of locations.

Isolated on a spit of land abutting the Poulaphuca Reservoir, it appears that here is a village that grew without a hinterland. So, how could this settlement come into existence in such an isolated location? The answer is, of course, that it didn't. Maps drawn in the nineteenth century show Valleymount located on high ground between the well-populated valleys of the Kings and Liffey rivers.

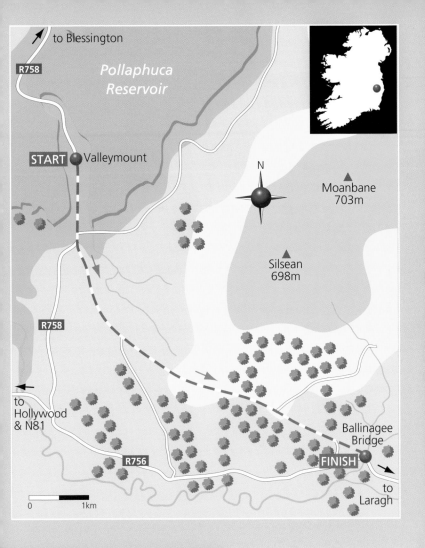

to Blessington

R758

Pollaphuca
Reservoir

START ● Valleymount

N

Moanbane
703m

Silsean
698m

R758

to
Hollywood
& N81

R756

Ballinagee
Bridge

FINISH ●

to
Laragh

0   1km

St Kevin's Way

In the 1930s it was decided to create a huge reservoir and hydroelectric scheme by damming the Poulaphouca Waterfall on the River Liffey and thereby drowning 5,600 acres around Valleymount. These days, it beggars the imagination to consider the amount of hoops, in the form objections and planning appeals, that would need to be jumped through in order to accomplish such an ambitious endeavour. Those

St Joseph's Church, Valleymount, the alternative start point for pilgrim walkers on St Kevin's Way.

were simpler times, however, and seemingly without any great fuss, over seventy families were displaced from the valley and rehoused elsewhere.

So I was to discover that an alternative start point for St Kevin's Way was located in the village of Valleymount and would require a visit and an exploration of the surrounding countryside. With high summer bursting out all around me, I therefore pointed my wheels in the direction of west Wicklow. Passing through Ballymore Eustace, I find the Kildare village is neatly flower strewn and comes across with an air of unostentatious prosperity, putting me in mind of England's Cotswolds villages. In many ways, it typifies the new affluence that has spread from booming Dublin to the surrounding counties like a rapidly melting ice cream.

Beyond, it's over a bridge, which crosses the Poulaphuca reservoir at a narrow point to provide a link with the Boystown Peninsula. Here, the road skirts the waterside delightfully and offers a memorable prospect over the vast, still waters to the serenity of the Wicklow Mountains beyond. Another bridge then conveys me to the village proper, which rather disappointingly turns out to be something of a ribbon development that offers little in the way of lakeside views. I had been told that the traditional start point of the pilgrim walk to Glendalough is outside St Joseph's Church, so I stop there as a summer shower dampens the street.

The church was built, like many such, during the period of Catholic resurgence in the early part of the nineteenth century. What makes it distinctive, however, is the fabulously pointless façade that was added around 1835. Latin American in its architectural style, it is the legacy, apparently, of returned emigrants. Certainly, it is unusual enough to have drawn the attention of the nineteenth-century faithful to the local house of God, but I can't help wondering how such an ostentatious edifice was funded amid the austerity of pre-Famine Ireland.

Outside the church, a small group of what seem clearly to be pilgrim walkers are about to set off. Their accents suggest that they come from Northern Ireland. When I enquire if they are heading for Glendalough, their leader replies in the affirmative. Always curious about pilgrim motivation, I ask what attracted them to this particular journey, but am rewarded only with: 'our friends recommended it and we thought it would be a nice walk.'

As they head off through the soft rain on their voyage of discovery, I nip inside the church in the hope of letting the shower pass. The interior conforms to a more typically vernacular style of architecture. Most arresting is the fine collection magnificent windows, including some containing unmistakably deep blue hues, signifying the work of the renowned artist, Harry Clarke.

Then it's back out into the continuing rain and the beginning of my pilgrim journey. At first, I had thought Valleymount a rather incongruous departure point for a pilgrimage dedicated to St Kevin, considering that tradition holds that the saint journeyed across the Wicklow Gap to Glendalough having overnighted, not near Valleymount, but in a cave outside Hollywood. But this is to ignore pilgrims coming afterwards. The

View over Poulaphuca Reservoir from St Kevin's Way.

Pilgrim walkers approaching Ballinagee Bridge on St Kevin's Way.

Camino de Santiago was, after all, not created by the feet of the Saint James, but by the footfall of medieval pilgrims coming to gain indulgences by visiting his grave after his body has been transported from the Holy Land. So it is entirely credible, and indeed probable, that large numbers of pilgrims coming from the north midlands would have availed of this route for their penitential journey to visit the last resting place of St Kevin.

Having satisfied myself that I am genuinely following the footsteps of pilgrims past, I set off down the village street. As the rain finally relents, I begin wondering how the beginning of this route will compare with the rather meandering start from Hollywood. The first waymarker denoting Slí Naomh Caoimhín (St Kevin's Way) appears at three-way junction just outside the village where a sign points left for Ballyknockan. Beyond the grassy mound covering an old sweat house on the left, whispers of forgotten history. Reaching back to Celtic times, the forerunner of the modern sauna was heated to a high temperature by an open fire and, by those who could endure the intense heat, was considered a cure for joint pain. It would have been, I reflect, an ideal way for weary pilgrims to chill out from their demanding journey, but I have no way of knowing if this is the reason for its existence.

A waymarker now directs me uphill on a public road. The route retains, nevertheless, the feel of a genuine pilgrim path and immediately puts me in mind of some sections of the Spanish Camino. My map shows a cross-inscribed stone located somewhere to the right of the route. I keep an eye out for this as an authentication of the spiritual past but fail to set eyes on it.

As I ascend, great vistas open up to the left and tumble down across sheep-strewn pastures to the watery expanse of Poulaphuca Reservoir. Slim and toned, a jogger suddenly glides past and immediately has me counting the odds that he also is heading for Glendalough. Concluding this is unlikely, I gain the high point of the route, which begins descending in the nature of a giant parabola. Expansive prospects now open up to my right over the serene Wicklow Gap and then south to Table and Conavalla mountains, with the peeping head of Lugnaquilla creeping above the horizon.

Sweeping easily down towards Ballinagee Bridge, I get the unmistakeable impression that here is a trail that is determined to take me somewhere. The resonance of a genuine pilgrim journey is amplified by the Northern Irish group ambling determinedly ahead with their hats and staffs and raincapes.

Soon, they disappear from view where the route swings left and enters a forest. I enter behind them. Trees make our world more three-dimensional and, as if to order, the sun emerges to dapple the woodlands from the canopy above. Now it's down a rough, unpoetic firebreak, which I imagine becomes very soft in wet weather. A firmer trail follows, leading through a wooden gate that carries a rather abstruse sign reading 'no shooting previous permission withdrawn', which must, I muse, be good news for the local fauna at least.

Beyond, the trail takes us to the Ballinagee River, where a right turn through a young plantation of mixed forestry deposits me on the road beside Ballinagee Bridge. This is the point where the Valleymount Spur joins the main pilgrim path from Hollywood and is my destination for today. I sit down and watch as the Northern group cross the bridge and then disappear up a forest road on the left.

In the warm sunshine I relax and enjoy the pleasant, gurgling sound of running water. A couple of tattooed young men – walkers or new age pilgrims? – stroll past. Then, a group of six appear and they are definitely doing the penitential route for they enquire how far it is to Glendalough. When I tell them it will take about another 3½ hours they seem initially crestfallen but nevertheless continue onwards with a cheery wave.

This gives me an opportunity to sit back and compare the virtues of the main route from Hollywood with those of the Valleymount spur. The path from Hollywood certainly resonates more with the imprint of St Kevin and makes for a delightful beginning. However, the meandering start and 2km walk along the busy R756, without the benefit of a hard shoulder, undoubtedly diminishes the experience. The Valleymount route offers a less direct connection with the life of St Kevin and is almost entirely along public roads. Mostly, however, the roads on the spur are extremely quiet and in many ways redolent of the Camino of St James. Taking all factors into account, I conclude that the more direct nature of the walk and the quieter, safer roads means my preference would strongly be for the Valleymount start.

11

KILCOMMON
PILGRIM LOOP | County Tipperary

OVERVIEW Ancient paths meandering the slopes of a mythical mountain offer a tangible connection to how the people of Slieve Felim have expressed the need for spirituality since pagan times.

SUITABILITY This is an easy route following well-maintained tracks with a total ascent of just 170m. It is, however, wet in places around the Bilboa River so good waterproof boots are a definite requirement.

GETTING THERE From Limerick take the N7 for Dublin and then the R50, signposted Newport. Continue through the villages of Newport and Rear Cross until the Cross Bar appears on the left. Go left immediately onto a minor road that leads directly to Kilcommon village. The trailhead is outside the Community Centre where there is ample parking. (R900 600).

TIME. Allow about 2 hours to complete the loop and about another 1½ hours to ascend Mauherslieve.

DISTANCE 7km.

HIGHEST ALTITUDE Mauherslieve (543m) but a summit excursion is not a required part of the Pilgrim Loop.

MAP OSi *Discovery Series* 59.

A feature of modern life is the phenomenon known as 'the death of distance'. Railways, cars and latterly airplanes have shrunk our planet to a size where we can travel almost anywhere in a couple of days. As citizens of this global village, we are apt to forget that, not so long ago, a night spent away from home was rare indeed and the limit of most journeys was a half-day walk from one's fireside. In those harsher times,

distances were very real indeed and the next valley often seemed another country. But for those who did travel, the slow pace carried its own reward – a deep interaction with the landscape that is impossible nowadays as we hurtle past at 100km/h.

Today, I won't be hurtling anywhere, however, but will instead savour the Tipperary countryside at a pace that was universal to ordinary folk until well into the last century. I am among a group invited to ramble a pilgrim trail with pagan origins that is being footed today as a celebration for National Pilgrim Paths Day.

Set in the valley of the Bilboa River and surrounded on all sides by uplands, Kilcommon is a neatly maintained village that valiantly retains its 'olde-worlde' charm. Starting from the village, Kilcommon Pilgrim Loop follows ancient paths that were stoically trod by generations of upland folk.

When I arrive, a large group is already waiting in the attractively laid-out village for what will be a brief opportunity to liberate ourselves temporarily from the immediacies and pressures of modern life. Some

Celebrating Pilgrim Paths Day on the Kilcommon Pilgrim Loop.

while away the time by exploring the nearby prayer garden, where a long-standing tradition of pilgrimage continues unabated, with thousands of the faithful still gathering here in reverence on summer days. Soon, we are greeted by Father Dan Woods, a local priest with a long record of service to the community and an abiding passion for its history and folklore. With rich vivacity he explains that the first paved road reached Kilcommon in 1831 and up to that time all travel was by a dense network of Mass paths. These not only helped maintain 'an unbroken chain of simple faith in the area', but were also a necessary lifeline facilitating all other human interactions.

He then introduces the new Mythic Map for the Pilgrim Loop Walk, which is mounted in the Windwalker annex of the Community Centre. This piece of artwork represents the seven sacred portals of the Loop, referencing the heritage of the Slieve Felims from pre-Christian to modern times. It was commissioned from the artist Desmond Dillon who spent time exploring the Kilcommon Pilgrim Loop Walk and working with the children of the local primary school.

Then, with the infectious energy of a man half his years, Father Woods leads us from Kilcommon Community Centre by following a minor road for a short distance before swinging right to traverse low-lying lands adjacent to the Bilboa River. It is April and already the rich aromas of the countryside marinate the air and the walking is pleasant, for every effort has been made to ease your passing. We follow purple

Cross-inscribed Mass rock at Laghile.

arrows through an SAC (Special Area of Conservation), traversing neatly constructed paths before crossing a couple of locally made bridges that fit snugly into the surrounding landscape.

Reaching a tarmac roadway, Father Woods leads us right and then left to join a woodland track. This soon swings right to follow a fence before crossing a forest roadway. Onwards and upwards to gain another forest road where a right turn has us traversing the lower skirts of deeply mythological Mauherslieve (Mother Mountain). Father Woods chooses this point to explain that the mountain is referred to by local people as Moher Clea and was in pre-Christian times reputedly an abode of the pagan goddess, Ebhleen.

Shortly afterwards, there is a choice to foot it upwards on a more demanding track to the mountain's lonesome crest by following an arrow marked 'Mauherslieve summit'. This points invitingly left onto a forest pathway that meanders upwards while initially offering a firm stone base before deteriorating into a soft peatland trail. Soon after, the arrows marked 'summit' go right and later up through a forest firebreak to reach open mountainside.

Here, it is right and gently upwards to reach the sensuously curved shoulders of Mauherslieve (543m) that do much to justify its Gaelic translation as 'Mother Mountain'. The top is crowned by a partially collapsed prehistoric burial cairn known locally as the Terrot. This is surmounted by an incongruous-looking trig point, which is a good place to linger, as the view is redolent of, but in many ways more impressive than that offered by Armagh's famous Ring Dyke around Slieve Gullion.

Like most constructers of mountaintop cairns, the builders clearly wanted to emphasise the cairn's importance by using the power of the most elevated place to invoke the reverence and respect of those residing in the valleys below. Certainly, Mauherslieve was well chosen, as it is a centrally situated summit offering a great vista over a surrounding ring of hills and was until relatively recently the scene of a devotional pattern-day pilgrimage on 29 June each year. This date is unusual and marks the feast of Ss Peter and Paul, instead of the more widely celebrated Festival of Lughnasa, which took place on the nearest Sunday to 1 August.

This being Pilgrim Paths Day, no expedition is planned to Mauherslieve summit. Leaving the forest roadway we descend instead through shady woodland to reach a country lane. From the lane, we cross a stile into a field that falls away to gain a roadway. Here, the arrows point left, but a 200m detour to the right through a gateway takes us to the ancient Mass rock at Laghile and the centre point of the Pilgrim Paths Day celebrations.

Sitting around waiting for the ceremony to begin, I can't help but reflect that this is the perfect place to ignite the imagination about life

Trig point on the summit of Mauherslieve.

eighteenth-century Ireland. Here, it is easy to conjure up visions of simple but devout people – whose lives were regulated not by clocks but by the rhythms of the countryside – coming from the surrounding hills to kneel and pray on the rough, wet grass while lookouts watched for the approach of hostile forces. In common with pilgrims from time immemorial, they would thus have fulfilled the universal human desire to reinforce community identity by sharing a mutual spiritual understanding.

Appropriate reflections and spiritual readings are then led by Father Anthony Keane of Glenstal Abbey to the sound of sweet musical accompaniment before it is time to complete the remainder of the route by following the purple arrows by quiet lanes and small fields once so typical of pre-EU rural Ireland. Initially, it's downhill along a by-road before crossing a field and another road to traverse wettish lands in the floodplain of the Bilboa River. Our walk concludes with a 700m ramble along a quiet road past a small riverside park to the trailhead in Kilcommon village.

12

THE RIAN BÓ PHÁDRAIG |
Counties Tipperary/Waterford

OVERVIEW One of the most challenging and varied of the Irish Pilgrim Paths, the Rian offers the reward of a genuine away-from-it-all upland experience. When the ongoing upgrade of the route is complete, the variety and challenge on offer should make it one of Ireland's finest pilgrim outings.

SUITABILITY Demanding walk requiring reasonable fitness along with clothing and footwear suitable for high-level hillwalking. As the route follows high mountain terrain, navigation skills will be required in mist.

GETTING THERE The south Tipperary village of Ardfinnan is located due south of Cahir and west of Clonmel. Begin your walk from outside the Holy Family Catholic Church. (S078 174).

FINISH Either Lismore or Mount Melleray Abbey. Since there is no public transport from either location to Ardfinnan, you will need to arrange a lift or organise a taxi.

TIME 6 hours (Ardfinnan to Lismore); 5 hours (Ardfinnan to Mount Melleray).

DISTANCE 23 km (Ardfinnan to Lismore); 20km (Ardfinnan to Mount Melleray).

HIGHEST ALTITUDE Bottleneck Pass (537m).

MAP OSi *Discovery Series* 74.

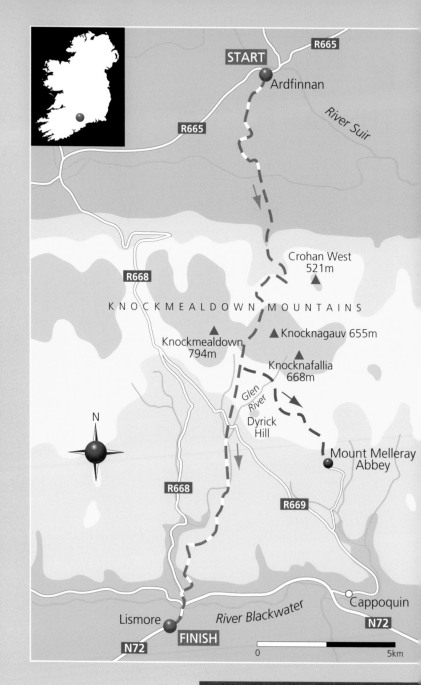

START

R665

Ardfinnan

River Suir

R665

Crohan West
521m

K N O C K M E A L D O W N   M O U N T A I N S

R668

▲ Knocknagauv 655m

▲ Knockmealdown
794m

▲ Knocknafallia
668m

Glen River

N

Dyrick
Hill

Mount Melleray
Abbey

R668

R669

Cappoquin

Lismore

River Blackwater

N72

FINISH

N72

0   5km

The Rian Bó Phádraig

I magine celebrating Ireland's national feast day not in March but in high summer. Hard to visualise the occasion accompanied by bikinis, barbeques and beach badminton? Yet it could have happened, for 24 July is the commemoration day for an early Irish saint with credentials comparable to St Patrick. Regarded by many historians as holding a strong claim to the title of first Irish Christian missionary, St Declan is, nevertheless, virtually unknown outside his native County Waterford.

The murky world of medieval Church politics has much to answer for here. It allowed the deeply venerated saint of the Deise, the ancient Gaelic name for Waterford, to fade from public consciousness when the northern Church rose to prominence. History was then adroitly written to suit the needs of the time, with Patrick, the first Bishop of Armagh, promulgated above Declan of Ardmore as the first evangeliser of the Irish people. Despite his ensuing obscurity, a robust tradition reaches down through the centuries that refers to Waterford's patron saint Christianising much of the south and making many journeys by chariot from Ardmore to the royal seat at Cashel.

Now St Declan's legacy is being reclaimed, with pilgrim walkers coming again to journey in his footsteps. The path he is reputed to have used to cross the Knockmealdown Mountains has now been revitalised and waymarked, so it was in good spirits that I roved out on a summer morning from Ardfinnan Church to reacquaint myself with St Declan's journey.

Following signs for the Tipperary Heritage Way, I was soon ambling along a quiet country road with grass adorning the middle, while enjoying memorable views of the Knockmealdown Mountains flowing seamlessly together like a giant emerald necklace. Stopping briefly to explore Ladysabbey, a former Carmelite House, whose early origins have been lost in the mists of antiquity, I found the building had almost entirely conceded to ivy.

Continuing to a T-junction, where in ancient times the route went directly ahead, I was obliged to go right, then left and follow this road to the left again before regaining it. This put me in mind of the first occasion I came this way. Chancing upon a weather-beaten man with a Waterford accent I was immediately questioned about the nature of my destination. 'St Declan's Way to Lismore over Bottleneck Pass,' I replied with, perhaps, a hint of hubris 'No, you're not,' was the deflating reply. 'But isn't this the ancient pilgrim path through the Knockmealdowns?' I asked. 'Yes, but it's not St Declan's Way. It's the Rian Bó Phádraig, the track of St Patrick's cow. St Declan's Road runs from Ardmore to Lismore.'

Historically, he was right of course. St Declan's Way is a relatively modern construction based on a number of ancient trails including Bóthar na Naomh and Declan's Road, which Declan is presumed to have used on his journeys from Ardmore to Cashel. Today, I was traversing the Rian, a prehistoric trail that whispered of an intriguing history. Legend holds that it takes its name from a cow owned by St Patrick. This giant bovine was grazing placidly on the rich pastures south of Ardfinnan when a thief from County Waterford abducted her calf and bore it over the Knockmealdown Mountains. In anger, the cow charged up the mountain and created a huge furrow with its horns as it pursued the stolen calf, which could just as easily suggest the creation of the route is actually attributable to the presence of St Patrick.

But just then facts seemed unimportant, for what had drawn me, like countless others over the years, was the long-standing tradition of a spiritual journey to Ardmore. Marked only the previous Easter by the footfall of 130 pilgrims, the Knockmealdown Pilgrim Path remains enduring proof of the restless human search for intangible values that materialism inevitably leaves unsatisfied.

Back in the present, it was down a pebbled path to cross the River Tar by a footbridge, before following what is known locally as the Bóthar Caoch (the Blind Road) to reach the main Clogheen–Newcastle road. Directly opposite, a cul-du-sac road led on to a pleasant, if sometimes wet, woodland trail. At the next intersection the arrows pointed to a T-junction where a finger sign indicated that it was 4km to the Liam Lynch Monument. This 20m-high memorial in the form of an Irish round tower was erected in 1935 and stands sentinel to the memory of Liam Lynch, chief of staff of the republican forces during the Irish Civil War. It marks the location where Lynch was fatally wounded on 10 April 1923 in a gun battle with the Free State Army. This incident marked the effective end of the very bloody and bitter Irish Civil War.

The pilgrim path went right from this T-junction before parting company shortly afterwards with the Tipperary Heritage Way by heading in a direction contra to the yellow arrows for St Declan's Way. These conveyed me left and uphill to a right turn over a concrete bridge and then upwards for almost 3km while still on a sympathetic track. The next section then came as something of an unpleasant shock. Yellow arrows pointed left and up a steep and eroded zigzagging forest path, known locally as Na Staighrí ('the stairs') to gain open mountainside.

Unforgiving terrain now marked my ascent (right) towards Bottleneck Pass, but then pilgrim trails aren't meant to be sanitised and, unlike medieval penitents, I was comfortably shod in mountain boots. The compensation for effort was a feeling of wildness all around in a pristine, upland wilderness.

This had me reflecting upon how unaltered the surrounding landforms have remained since the era of St Declan, when a blanket of grey dropped around me like a giant theatre curtain. Suddenly, I became disconnected from the present as my world dissolved to opaque mist as it must have done regularly for pilgrims past. It was me against the elements in a surreal, timeless realm, and as if to test my resolve, the weather immediately turned foul.

Despite a soubriquet more suited to a John Wayne western, Bottleneck Pass is actually an unremarkable place although it does denote the county boundary between Counties Tipperary and Waterford. Denied even the mistiest glimpse of the surrounding landforms, I tarried only long enough in the biting cold to wonder how Declan's chariot could possibly have surmounted the unforgiving terrain of the high Knockmeadowns before descending what was now a better-defined track. Soon after, the mist parted and the rain cleared to reveal outrageously photogenic views over the meandering River Blackwater to coastal Ardmore and the silvery southern ocean beyond. Now, I could make out the dreamy outline of the renowned Cistercian Abbey of Mount Melleray. At that moment, it seemed as if it rose above the surrounding woodlands like a 21st-century beacon of tranquillity and security in an otherwise turbulent and confusing world.

Originally Melleray Abbey was located in Brittany and housed mostly overseas monks, including many from Ireland. When foreign clergy were expelled from France in 1830, the Melleray-based community members from these islands fled to Ireland. France's loss was Ireland's gain, for a new and highly productive Mount Melleray Abbey sprang up at this austerely beautiful location among the foothills of the Knockmealdown Mountains.

Reflecting on the timeless nature of this ancient walkway I passed right of outlying Dyrick Hill as the slope eased. The heathery track then became more penitential and ill-defined in places before joining a fence that conveyed me to a farm lane leading to the R669 near Gloungarrif Bridge.

Directly opposite, a solitary arrow for St Declan's Way indicated south along a rural road. After this there were no more reassuring arrows, so I resorted to taking out my Ordnance Survey map to work out the best route through a labyrinth of minor roads. Comparing my map to the one contained in a book titled *Along St Declan's Way* by Siobhan Lincoln, I went right at the first junction and kept straight at the next. A little further on, Lincoln shows the Rian diving left and across country, but I found no indication of where. So I just continued walking the rather mundane public road, which came as something of a let-down after the sublime crossing of the Knockmealdowns.

Mount Melleray Abbey.

Joining the main Lismore–Cahir Road beside the entrance to the Ballyrafter House Hotel, a fifteen-minute walk then takes me beneath the imposing Gothic ramparts of the Duke of Devonshire's residence at Lismore Castle to gain the town centre. Beautifully located beneath wooded hills on the banks of the River Blackwater, Lismore was once an important centre of learning with students coming to study here from all over Europe including, apparently, the future King Alfred the Great. Today, Lismore is probably best known as the birthplace of travel writer Dervla Murphy and for its annual Festival of Travel Writing which takes place each June. Certainly, the built environment seems the perfect backdrop to such an event for it immediately strikes me how well deserving Lismore is of its status as an Irish heritage town.

Passing by Lismore House Hotel, which declares itself the oldest purpose-built hotel in Ireland, I head in for a welcome coffee in the cosy comfort of the Spire Café. Here, I reflect that the rebirth of the Rian Bó Phádraig, despite its rather disappointing last section (which can be avoided by diverting to Mount Melleray), remains proof that the past never truly dies, but returns sooner or later to reconnect us with our heritage.

Alternative Route

If you want to avoid the long road walk to Lismore while enjoying the perfect pilgrim finish, you might consider this shorter alternative route, which is actually my preference: follow the Rian as described until you gain the south side of Bottleneck Pass. At S068 074, traverse left to reach the Rough Glen River (S080 069) where two streams coalesce. Here, the waters descend in a couple of small cascades at a point marked by a few skeletal thorn bushes that have been stripped by countless winter storms. A tiny canal, laboriously dug by industrious monks, takes water from the Rough Glen River, while presenting the baffling illusion that it is actually flowing uphill. Known locally as The Source, it was built to supply Melleray Abbey with fresh water. These days it is mainly used as a handrail by walkers crossing a trackless mountainside when mist has descended on the uplands.

The final section of the pilgrim journey to Mount Melleray Abbey.

Walkers following The Source while celebrating Pilgrim Paths Day.

Follow The Source across open mountainside, to a stile at S082 062. Beyond, a rough track leads to a well-surfaced forest roadway. Then it's left and straight through a four-way junction and a descent right at the next four-way junction. Just before reaching a large turning circle, a stony path goes right and down past a ruined dwelling and then follows the signs for Melleray Abbey along pleasant sylvan paths. Then what better way to finish a pilgrim journey than by arriving on foot to the lovely cut-stone building of the renowned Melleray monastery? Here, generations of Cistercian monks have provided multitudes with a retreat from the insanity of modern living while themselves savouring the riches of owning nothing.

13

ARDMORE PILGRIM PATH |
County Waterford

OVERVIEW Shortest and easiest of the Irish pilgrim routes, the Ardmore Pilgrim Path provides, nevertheless, rich reward for minimum effort. The coastal views are truly spectacular, there is strangely poignant sense of disappearing history and a delicious feeling throughout the walk that something new to explore will crop up around every corner.

SUITABILITY Relatively easy outing, following minor roads and green tracks. Care required when traversing the cliff-side path.

GETTING THERE From the N25, (main Cork–Waterford Road) take the R673 south to Ardmore.

TIME About 70 minutes of leisurely walking, but allow more time for exploring the pilgrim sites en route.

DISTANCE 4km.

MAP OSi *Discovery Series* 82, but not really necessary as the walk is well signposted.

I f history consists of stories that later generations agree to tell about the past, then Ardmore has done much to inspire story making. Such tales take us deep into the mindset of the societies that produced them and here Ireland's earliest saint provided the seed corn for the mythologies that have sustained and bonded local communities since Christianity's earliest dawning in Ireland.

Born into a royal family of the Deise Muman, who ruled southeast Munster, he was taught by a local scholar and holy man named Dioma. Seeing a pagan land around him and wishing for a different Ireland, Declan travelled to Rome on a personal journey of enlightenment.

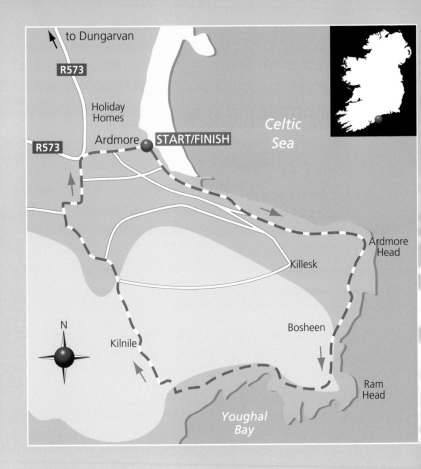

Ardmore Pilgrim Path

Consecrated a bishop, he returned to Ireland resolved to spend the remainder of his life preaching the gospel. En route, he is reputed to have encountered St Patrick on his outward journey to study in Rome, which, if true, is proof positive that Declan's evangelical mission to Ireland predated the Patrician one.

The agreed story that tradition has bequeathed of the relationship between the two saints recounts Patrick coming to Ireland as principal evangelist. He then emphasised this dominance by confirming Declan as Bishop of the Deise at a synod in Cashel. The early Christian period is, of course, an era when facts have become elaborately intertwined

Panoramic view of the walk's starting point at Ardmore village.
(www.johnfoleyimages.com)

with emotion, so whether the above account is true or not, one detail is certain: Declan's mission, unlike Patrick's, remained a local one, confined mostly to the area surrounding the monastery he founded at Ardmore.

Obliged to play an evangelical second fiddle to Patrick at national level, Declan remained supreme in his south Munster heartlands with Patrick, wisely perhaps, eschewing the Deise on his Irish mission. Revered through the intervening centuries as the highest-profile and most venerated saint of modern County Waterford, Declan lives on in the local memory when his feast day is celebrated enthusiastically with a week-long pattern in Ardmore each July.

Inexplicably, I had never been to this Waterford village, and was, therefore, anticipating my icebreaker visit with mild excitement. A former winner of the Irish Tidy Towns Competition that proudly boasts an expansive sandy beach and a vibrant artistic community, Ardmore promised much and didn't disappoint. It's a sunless, autumnal day when I arrive, yet the place exudes unpretentious prosperity alongside stay-a-while charm. Needing no second bidding to tarry in such a laid-back ambience, I head into the White Horse Restaurant where I am charmed by delicious seafood chowder that simply shouts of wild Atlantic origins.

Down the street is the start point for my walk, which begins from the waterside opposite the Catholic Church and leads west along the promenade to gain the rocky shoreline bookending Ardmore's spacious strand. My curiosity is arrested here by St Declan's Rock lying just beyond the sea wall. Legend tells us, Declan was sailing back from Rome and searching urgently for a site to build a monastery. Guided by a large floating stone, which carried a bell on top, he was led to Ardmore and there constructed his monastic enclosure. At low tide, it is apparently possible to crawl under the stone as a cure for many ailments, but with the weather deteriorating, I decide this is not the time to interrogate the legend further and so I head uphill instead.

At the high point, I pause outside what at first glance seems an austere post-modernist building. Inside, I have been told, is one of Ireland's most spectacularly located boutique hotels and it seems like a pity to pass by without calling in for a cuppa. Further justification comes in the form of a sea fog, which has rolled in from the Celtic Sea and subsumed the landscape in a blanket of misty surrealism and so I nip in for a coffee and scone in the hope that the mist will clear later.

Sitting on a seaside veranda, my gaze is drawn out over the watery grey light above the ocean and I try to imagine the moment Declan's little ship arrived in Ardmore. The stories of the early Christian saints have, of course, been extravagantly reshaped to match later societal ideals, but at that languorous moment of my pilgrim journey, I would only have been half surprised to see a bell-topped rock and ghostly ship emerging silently from the mist.

Back outside, the sea fog is, if anything, denser, so working with the maxim that early pilgrims must often have experienced immeasurably worse, I cross a stile conveying me into the area where Declan created a rich geometry of spirituality. Pilgrim path markers lead me first to the ruins of Declan's Hermitage and a holy well, where the saint is reputed to have performed many baptisms before retiring here to pray during his latter years. This site remains a place of pilgrimage, particularly on 24 July, the feast of St Declan; as evidence of this, the well is adorned with dozens of votive offerings.

The route now wanders along the eastern edge of the peninsula, with great eerie declivities dropping to my left. Soon, the rusting remains of the *Samson* are just discernible through ethereal mist. This crane ship came unstuck from her tow while being taken to Malta and fetched up, without causing loss of life, at the base of the cliffs beneath Ardmore Head. Here it has become – like the *Plassey* wreck on Inisheer – an unlikely, but popular tourist attraction.

The pilgrim path now meanders languidly around Ram Head. In good weather this area apparently offers a sensational vista over Youghal Bay and along the east Cork coastline, but today, all I see is a great swirl of opaque clag. There are, however, two coastal lookout stations. The tallest served as a watchtower in case of a Napoleonic invasion, while the second is far less salubrious and consists of a small bunker-like structure built as a lookout upon the outbreak of the Second World War.

Beyond, a stone structure built over a spring has all the appearance of an ancient holy well. Locally referred to as Father O'Donnell's Well it was, I am later somewhat disappointed to discover, actually built in 1928 by one T. P. O'Rahilly of Limerick, who believed strongly in the curative power of the waters issuing here.

St Declan's Hermitage.

Following the pilgrim markers inland near the local soccer pitch, I have a feeling of being strangely uncoupled from the world as the renowned Ardmore round tower emerges from the swirling mist, rising gun-barrel straight to a majestic 30m. Obviously, Declan had an architect's eye when it came to choosing his monastic site, for even in the eerie twilight, it is clear that his monastery was designed to dominate landscape and seascape, making his Christian message impossible to ignore.

Entering what is generally regarded as Ireland's oldest Christian site, I bump into an unpretentious local man eager to discuss the (mixed) fortunes of the Waterford hurling team. Subject finally exhausted, we then segue to discussion of the locality where he proves a mine of information. He speaks of the many shipwrecks along this unforgiving coastline and then points to a large grave in a corner of the monastic site. This, he tells me, represents the last resting place of crew members from the SS *Ary* which foundered in a storm during the 'freezing cold winter' of 1947.

Drifting in lifeboats the crew died one by one of exposure, leaving a Polish man, Jan Dorucki, the sole survivor. After two days the lifeboat came ashore up the coast at Old Parish Cliffs. Unsurprisingly, Jan was now in a poor state, but managed somehow to scramble upwards and then drag himself to a farmhouse. From here, he was transferred to Dungarvan Hospital, where his legs were amputated due to the effects of frostbite. The bodies of his companions were washed ashore and now lie buried in a communal grave beneath small anchors, which were laid on their last resting place by the local community.

Before departing he tells me that the oldest building on the site is St Declan's Oratory, within which lie the remains of the saint. There is no entry to the oratory, so I can't investigate this claim, but poking around the Romanesque cathedral brings its own reward. I find it boasts a lavishly ornate gable, depicting stories from the bible and two standing stones inscribed with ogham, the earliest form of Gaelic writing.

The roofless cathedral at Ardmore.

Ardmore round tower in mist.

Outside, for some reason I cannot articulate, I feel drawn towards the base of the great round tower that today fades tantalisingly into the mist above. Agreement has not been reached among historians as to the exact purpose of these distinctly Celtic edifices, but in school I remember being assured they were places of refuge for people and valuables during the era of Viking raids. Gazing upwards at the great tower, this seems an unlikely explanation. The ease with which the defenders could be burned out seems undeniable. Certainly, were bloodthirsty Vikings to appear on the horizon at that moment, my instinct would not be to rush inside the claustrophobic confines of the tower, but would instead involve legging it cross-country at the greatest possible speed in the opposite direction.

Later, as I head downhill from the monastic site, it strikes me that, whatever their purpose – symbolic or practical – we should be grateful to the builders of these great structures. Minimalist creations of the greatest beauty, their true wonder is that, for about 1,000 years, they have articulately spoken to succeeding generations about the extravagant flourishing of Irish culture in the period immediately prior to the Norman invasion.

It is raining enthusiastically by the time I regain the start point of the walk. As I prepare to drive away in the watery twilight, it occurs to me that nowhere else on my Irish pilgrim journey did the ghosts of the Christian past appear to linger so tangibly as at Ardmore. Early Christian monastic life as practised here, with its emphasis on simplicity, mindfulness and humility, still has lessons for us, it seems, even in the second decade of the twenty-first century.

14

MOUNT BRANDON
PILGRIM PATH | County Kerry

OVERVIEW Great in-and-out walk to one of Ireland's most majestic and revered mountains on a genuinely ancient pilgrim trail. You will enjoy majestic mountain and lake scenery while following a track that is reasonably well waymarked. The alternative descent, traversing west from the summit towards Brandon peak is not a recognised pilgrim trail as such but is described for experienced hillwalkers who wish to avoid retracing their steps to Faha and because it is a fine outing in itself.

SUITABILITY A there-and-back outing to Brandon's summit is not overly demanding and should present no real problems for even moderately experienced hillwalkers. The alternative descent is suitable only for hillwalkers with a full suite of upland skills.

GETTING THERE Take the main road (the N86) onto the Dingle Peninsula from Tralee and go straight ahead (on the R560) at the blink-and-you-miss-it village of Camp. Further on, follow the signs right for Mount Brandon and Cloghane. Keep going beyond Cloghane and then take the second left, which is signposted Mount Brandon. This leads up to the farmyard at Faha where limited parking is provided (Q493 120), your start/finish point.

TIME Allow 4 hours for an ascent and descent of Brandon. Allocate 6 hours for the full circuit that descends by the Garraneceol.

DISTANCE 8km approx. (extended route is 10km).

HIGHEST ALTITUDE Brandon Mountain (924m).

MAP OSi map of Mount Brandon, 1:25,000; OSi *Discovery Series* 70.

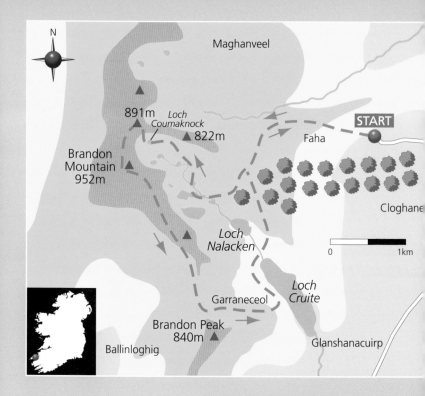

N

Maghanveel

891m
Loch Coumaknock
822m

Brandon
Mountain
952m

START

Faha

Cloghane

0   1km

Loch Nalacken

Loch Cruite

Garraneceol

Brandon Peak
840m

Ballinloghig

Glanshanacuirp

Mount Brandon

t is a journey that always fills me with pulse-raising anticipation. Once the unsightly roundabout-plagued roads through suburban Tralee are behind, I can't avoid an eager feeling of entering a place where time matters less. This is a landscape where globalised Ireland simply never turned up. Despite the pressures of mass tourism, the Dingle Peninsula remains defiantly unkempt, unpackaged and untamed. Shaped much like an index finger pointing at America, this is a land of improbably huge sea cliffs with unforgettable views while the hills topping the peninsula are indeed some of Ireland's finest. And the prince among these uplands is undoubtedly the elongated ridge that gambols erratically from Ireland's highest mountain pass to the ocean.

It is almost impossible for anyone to traverse the head of the Conor Pass without stopping to marvel at the relentlessly mournful landscape of wet fields, lonesome lakes and timeless mountains. And indeed the Brandon range overlooks a desolate topography that has thwarted man's

Brandon Bay as seen from Mount Brandon's Pilgrim Path.

best efforts for generations and thus created many sad stories of poverty and emigration. But these mountains also gaze upon many wonderfully austere places in an intricate landscape that is difficult to render productive, but captivating to explore. Here we have a treasure chest for those who enjoy strenuous legwork among superb hills adorned with many antiquities and a rich folklore.

Today, however, I eschew the attractions of the Conor Pass and beneath unwelcoming skies swing right from the tourist trail and head north for the serene village of Cloghane. Mind crackling, as always, with anticipation for what lies ahead,

Marian shrine beside Mount Brandon's Pilgrim Path.

I continue to a small car park at Faha. Here, a chocolate-box-pretty farmhouse is neatly framed by the elegant sweep of the mystical Brandon range behind. Soon after, I head past the farmhouse to gain open mountainside and then follow one of Ireland's finest trails – the ancient Pilgrim Path to Mount Brandon's summit. The sense of pilgrimage is reinforced as the waymarked route passes a grotto dedicated to Our Lady of the Mountains. Then the well-worn path climbs steadily up a rather dull hill before contouring below the eastern extremity of the Faha Ridge.

I have been this way so many times that I should now be eligible for a Mount Brandon loyalty card. So I am not concerned by the relatively mundane landscape for I know that, like all the best mountains, Brandon reveals its secrets slowly. In its own good time, Brandon allows me a first glimpse of the superb Coumaknock, which has been gouged out by ice and water, with its morosely bare rock and string of paternoster lakes stretched upwards like the beads of a rosary. Traversing above this world of wonder, the track clings to the steep ground below the camel-back Faha Ridge, before intercepting the valley floor near its great northern headwall. Here, it initially seems there is no way up the steep rocky face – but fortunately it has one weakness in its defences, for a track labours upwards beneath a rising rocky face. This is the Becher's Brook of the route, and although not truly challenging, it requires some easy scrambling over user-friendly rocks to overcome some of the problems.

When all difficulties are finally behind, I step onto the Brandon Ridge proper where my eyes are now drawn to the spiky austerity of the Faha Ridge, which never fails to remind me of a great weather-ravaged ship, moored to the flanks of Brandon's stout eastern ramparts. Here I swing left and follow a well-trodden path that appears to reach down like a spindly arm from the summit to welcome the walker.

In a good mood, Brandon offers arresting views stretching from MacGillycuddy's Reeks all the way west to the staggeringly beautiful Blasket Islands and then north to the surreal outline of the Aran Islands. But such humours

View over the Paternoster lakes of Coumaknock from high on the pilgrim path to Mount Brandon.

are disappointingly rare, for Brandon is also well known as a mercurial mountain that mostly prefers to hide its handsome head in mist.

And so, while I have always loved the unforgettable views from Brandon's summit, the mountain rarely returns my ardour. Today is one of those occasions, for mist hangs around Ireland's highest piece of real estate outside the Iveragh Peninsula, like an unwelcome house guest. Alone on the summit and shivering in the black wind and spattering rain, I examine the remains of a ruined oratory beneath the summit cross. This is where St Brendan and his monks reputedly celebrated Mass before setting out on their voyage across the Atlantic in a currach.

Immediately this raises the question: was St Brendan the first European to reach the New World? Certainly, an ancient Latin text describes, with credible detail, a seven-year journey by the saint to the 'Isle of the Blessed', which could have been North America. Nobody can, of course, be certain if he succeeded in confronting the wild North Atlantic to reach the New World, but if he did, his achievement would far outshine, for its sheer audacity, anything achieved by Edmund Hillary, Ernest Shackleton or Neil Armstrong, and his appellation, 'the Navigator', was truly well earned.

Whether he counts as one of the world's greatest explorers or not, Brendan is certainly the dominant spiritual brand on the Dingle Peninsula with the generally ubiquitous St Patrick hardly getting a look-in. An old tale, obviously aimed at reinforcing the extent of this huge regard, tells that once, when he led a pilgrimage up Brandon, the saint forgot his missal. No problem, he just sent the word down the line of ascending pilgrims stretching all the way to the mountain foot and the book was then passed up to him. Whether this tale is true or not the reverential tradition on Brandon continues and is recreated on the last Sunday of July each year with a pilgrim climb for the celebration of Mass on the summit as part of Cloghane's apparently highly inclusive Festival of Lughnasa.

From the mountaintop I can, of course, retrace my steps to Faha. It is simply a matter of following the ascent path as it descends northwards until a sign points the route downwards to your right. The way down initially seems intimidating but it isn't really and surprisingly quickly walkers find themselves back on the floor of Coumaknock. From here, a rough trail, indicated by occasional arrows on the rock, contours left past some small lakes and then follows the wall of the coum to reach a high point. Now it is just a question of following a line of white poles back to the farmyard at Faha.

But simply to do this seems a wasted opportunity, for Brandon is a mountain with many more aces up its rugged sleeve. My favourite way down the east side of the Brandon range involves following first a fence south and then a wall along the broad crest of the ridge. Adrenalin addicts can choose to follow the apex of the ridge while enjoying memorable views over monstrous buttresses, scarifying gullies and enormous cliffs. As I descend, the mist clears and instantly the full glory of the Brandon range becomes apparent. The vista is immense but my eyes are, as always, drawn to one feature – the outrageously photogenic Blasket Islands shimmering in the western ocean.

After about 3km and immediately before the ground begins rising towards the summit of Brandon peak, a grassy ramp falls away steeply from the ridge to my left. Following this downwards, while being careful not to dislodge the many loose rocks, I find myself locked within the confines of a steep hanging valley. An enormous rockfall directly ahead provides the key to an impressive exit. Heading for this, I am soon hopping sweetly across the unbelievably immense stones of the Garraneceol boulder field. Every mountain is, of course, a work in progress and in Irish, Garraneceol (*Garrán ceol*) means 'terrible music'. The name was apparently coined by local people to describe the frightening sounds created by boulders as they were torn from the mountainside in high winds.

Beyond the Garraneceol, only one route of descent offers itself. On my right and close against the sheer north face of Brandon Peak, another easy ramp leads downwards to the austere waters of Lough Cruite ('Harp Lake'). I descend this and then follow the western shoreline of the lough north to reach an impressive waterfall. Here I cross a stream where it enters Cruite, immediately below the falls. It is then a question of ascending past some small lakes and waterfalls until I am reunited with the trail in from Faha.

Now I just follow the path back to Faha, where small groups of walkers are, despite the lateness in the day, heading upwards towards Mount Brandon's summit. A couple of English women want to know how far it is to the summit and we get into conversation. When I ask them what they intend doing in Ireland, they tell me they are doing Brandon, Croagh Patrick and maybe the Lough Derg pilgrimage. Never having met anyone attempting such a combination before, I ask them why they are doing this, while suspecting it may be to give thanks for some answer to prayer or, perhaps, to aid a good cause. The answer is surprisingly prosaic, however, for I am told, only half-jokingly, 'What we want is a backside like Kate's.' The Kate in question is surely the former Ms Middleton, I conclude, as I continue on down the mountain.

15

COSÁN NA NAOMH | County Kerry

OVERVIEW The Cosán na Naomh follows an ancient pilgrim route with a strong penitential tradition, finishing beneath one of Ireland's highest and most majestic mountains. The attractions here are rooted within people and place, and on foot is by far the best way to experience the elemental, skeletal topography of Corca Dhuibhne – the Dingle Peninsula – in its true dimensions.

SUITABILITY A relatively unchallenging but rather lengthy linear walk requiring transport at both ends.

GETTING THERE Follow the R559 west from Dingle. At Ventry, swing left for Ventry strand. The Cosán na Naomh is signposted from here (Q381 003).

FINISH Ballybrack (An Baile Breac) car park (Q434 095).

TIME Allow 4 to 5 hours to complete the Cosán. Please note, however, that this can easily morph into a very long day if time is spent exploring the many antiquities, historic buildings and religious sites along the route.

DISTANCE 18km.

HIGHEST ALTITUDE Reenconnell (274m).

MAP OSi *Discovery Series* 70.

I have always been drawn to the idea that the Irish countryside is a giant storybook eagerly seeking readers. Nowhere have I found this to be truer than west of Dingle. Here, beneath the huge skies of Corca Dhuibhne, exists a dense concentration of ring forts, souterrains, burial chambers and clocháns, or dry-stone huts. These form a vast literature in rock, awaiting

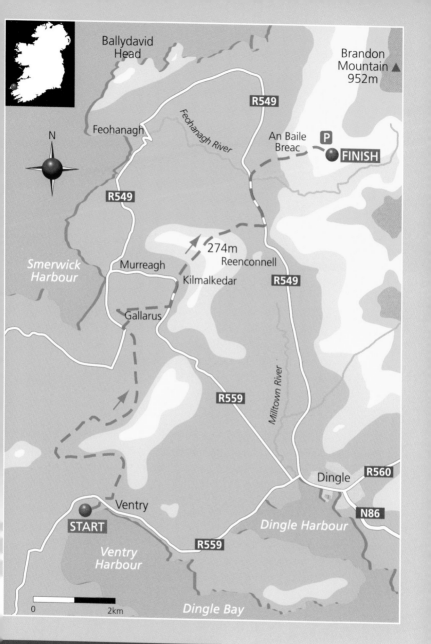

Cosán na Naomh

Ventry Beach, the unlikely starting point for Cosán na Naomh.

astute readers of the landscape with the skill to unlock the multilayered sagas of these ancient stones. And so, whenever I head out to the wind-sculpted, Irish-speaking region beyond Mount Brandon, I can't escape a feeling of regressing in time. Isolated for generations by mountain and ocean, the locals unhurriedly go about the traditional businesses of fishing and farming, troubled only by tour coaches and day trippers who — if they know what's good for them — follow the same clockwise route around the peninsula.

This morning, Dingle is heavy with pilgrims, but not ones heading for a redemptive trail. Instead they are queuing for another type of spiritual voyage, by seeking interaction with a dolphin that has made its home in Dingle Bay for three decades and in the process has become something of a superstar. Never one to throw a sickie or take a lazy beach day, the now ageing but still playful Fungie always rewards his fans with a performance, even in the worst of weather. There is even a souvenir shop near the waterfront named in his honour, along with an elegant bronze cast of a dolphin on the quayside.

Dingle itself is a well-known traffic pinch point with the town lying astride the only access road to parts further west. So the traffic is heavy as we head out beyond Dingle, and the land is overwhelmed by the vastness of the seascape that comes into view. This is the landscape David Lean used in his film *Ryan's Daughter* in 1970, kick-starting tourism in west Kerry in the process. Despite a stellar cast, the real star of the film, unsurprisingly, turned out to be the beguiling Kerry landscape. According to tradition, it was at Ventry that pilgrims arriving by boat came ashore, and then walked the Saint's Road (Cosán na Naomh) to Brendan's Oratory on Brandon's summit. (Today, however, the Cosán goes only to the foot of Brandon, with the Saint's Road, see chapter 12, going to the summit). So having made arrangements with family members for a later pick-up at Ballybrack (An Baile Breac) car park beneath Mount Brandon's benign west face, I head for the walk's start point.

I don't know what exactly I had been expecting at the trailhead. Another abbey, a beehive hut or perhaps a holy well? But this is one of a handful of days this summer that the sun has chosen to shine, and I am met with the hedonistic insouciance of a holiday beach, complete with surfers, kayakers, swimmers and even a group of bikini-clad sunbathers. There is a strong temptation to literally throw in the towel right now and veg out for the day on these magnificent sands.

My guide to the walk informs me that the beach wasn't always such. In the medieval period it was the most convenient landing place for sea-borne pilgrims journeying to Mount Brandon, while in prehistoric times a great battle reputedly took place here in which the ubiquitous Irish hero, Fionn Mac Cumhaill, defeated the emperor of the world.

Recalling the fortitude of pilgrims past, however, I resist temptation and pursue instead the signs for the Cosán, wooden posts marked with the emblem of a pilgrim with staff. I have read in the guidebook that the route is also marked by ancient stones with the 'cross of arcs', one of the principal symbols of pilgrimage in Ireland, and I am disappointed not to find any of these.

Initially, the way dallies along a series of pleasant back roads and fuchsia-rich lanes with many echoes from the past in the form of ring forts, monastic sites and a ruined medieval castle. After a short walk on the main Ventry–Ballyferriter road, the waymarkers lead right on a byroad that eventually transforms itself into a boreen offering stunning views over the Three Sisters' Peninsula and the rare scent of wild flowers perfuming the air. A little more road walking, and then a serene path through fields of abundant wild flowers puts me in contemplative mood, which inevitably means I lose the route. After faffing around for a bit I end up on a public road. Here, I chance upon someone who seems like a local man and, since this is the beating heart of the Kerry Gaeltacht, I decide I must make some kind of effort *as Gaeilge*. So I dust down my half-forgotten Irish and our conversation goes something like this.

'Dia duit.'
'How're you doing?'
'Lá maith atá againn inniu.'

'I suppose it's not so bad'.

Tá mé beagáinín caillte anois. An bhfuil a fhios agat cá bhfuil an shiúlóid Cosán na Naomh a chríochnaíonn in aice le Chnoc Bréanainn?'

''Twould be aisier to go by the road.'

'Tá sé sin fíor, ach tá mé ag lorg … Oh, never mind.'

As this stage I give up and revert to *Béarla.*

'Yes, that's ok. But, you see, I'd like directions for the cross-country route. I'm following the ancient pilgrim path to Mount Brandon.'

'Oh, suit yourself then. Just go back to the top of the lane. It's aisy to follow from there although the markers are hard to find.'

Then, with a final piece of advice as he points vaguely in the direction of Brandon – 'be careful, it's always bad up there' – he departs. Soon after, I discover why he advises a detour by road, for now the trail toils across a field of waist-high grass through which, like pilgrims of old, I must wade to reach Gallarus Oratory.

Now bereft of its original purpose as a community chapel, Gallarus has instead mutated into a modern place of worship for archaeology buffs. Startlingly uniform and puritanically unadorned, it is about the size of a large garden shed, but entirely built of unmortared stone with an apex roof that gives it the appearance of an upturned boat. However, it is in the interior twilight that it comes most to life. I gaze up in some awe at the sublimely corbelled roof, which is the true glory of the place and has not allowed even one drop of water to enter since the place was built aeons ago. How, I wonder, did these early medieval masons construct such a perfectly symmetrical arch of stone without it all collapsing on their unhelmeted heads?

Outside, I see a guide/information officer and decide to put this question to him, but this is Ireland, and so the preliminaries must be taken care of first. He wants to know where I'm from. Tipperary. And he? Athlone. Next he inquires why Lar (Tipperary hurler Lar Corbett) retired briefly last winter and seems surprised that I have no insider titbits about this from within the training camp. So I ask if Westmeath can overcome Kerry in the All-Ireland Football Championship on Sunday next. He thinks not, but wonders, in return, can Tipperary beat Kilkenny in hurling this year. Doubtful, I believe.

Some time later – actually quite a time later – we are ardently discussing the merits of Seamus Darby's decisive goal for Offaly in the 1982 All-Ireland Football Final – was it a push in the back? Then we are interrupted when a group of snap-happy Japanese arrive seeking information and our conversation ends abruptly. Later, over a coffee in the visitor centre, I realise I still have no idea how that roof stayed up. But I have learned something, though: Westmeath football has never been the same since the late, great Kerry man Páidí Ó Sé retired as manager.

A view of the Three Sisters and the Blasket Islands from
Cosán na Naomh. (Valerie O'Sullivan)

Gallarus Oratory.

Now it's a question of making my way for a short distance along a lane towards the striking eminence of Gallarus Castle. Outside, I read on the information board that the castle was built by the Fitzgerald family in the fifteenth century and has recently been restored. Technically, it is actually a tower house and according to the information, these were built by wealthy landowning families both as secure refuges and as status symbols. This is apparently one of the few surviving castles on the Dingle Peninsula.

This seems like an interesting visit and so I ask a workman who is leaving the building about having a look inside. 'Can't do that at present,' is his reply. When I ask why not, he answers, 'Money.' He explains there are no funds to pay a guide to look after the place. In response, I point out that this seems a bit penny wise and pound foolish. Surprisingly, he agrees with me but then adds, 'that's the way things are these days, no sense any more.' Then, with one final shake of his head, he drives off in his jeep. So it seems that huge amounts of money have been invested in this restoration only for it to be rendered meaningless for the want of the paltry sum to keep it manned during the summer season.

Down a lane, then right and left and right again on a public road now takes me to the most important ecclesiastical site in the area (see author's note at end of chapter). The centre point is Kilmalkedar's twelfth-century Hiberno-Romanesque church, which is thought to have been modelled on Cormac's Chapel at Cashel, County Tipperary, and is one of a number of stone-roofed churches to be found in Ireland. When I finally reach the sublimely located site, the church proves to be roofless but this seems unimportant for the place resonates with intangible mystery and stay-awhile charm. There is also an undoubted atmosphere of surreal mysticism that has moved an American couple to renew their commitment to each other in the ancient way by clasping fingers through a hole in a large standing stone.

When they depart I sit and soak up the solitude. And gazing out upon the next parish to America puts me in the mood to ruminate. I conclude that while the 'hidden Ireland' has now become something of a hackneyed old cliché dropped rather carelessly on many a nondescript location, Kilmalkedar ticks all the right uncommercial, unpackaged boxes for definition as a genuine place apart.

It is getting late in the day and the Reenconnell ridge now rises uninvitingly ahead like a large speed bump on the road to redemption. So I push on, following the waymarkers up towards a low point on the ridge. Great views open up around as I ascend through stone-wall-enclosed fields to the high point. For pilgrims past, this would have been the first close-up view over their promised land with the great rampart of the Brandon range filling the horizon. And directly below me is the defiantly untouristy Irish-speaking lands of Feohanagh – a charming backwater close to, but removed from, the intrusions of mass tourism.

Here, a rocky outcrop displays a recently discovered piece of rock art. Created as a perfect spiral motif, this artifact long predates Christian pilgrimage, and I can't help but wonder about the artist who long ago chanced this way. Why did he, or she, feel the urge to linger and create an eye-catching object of simple beauty that still speaks to us today? This is a question that must forever remain shrouded in the mists of time, so without a satisfactory answer, I rise and begin heading downhill.

On the descent, the terrain becomes rougher although it remains well waymarked, but I now discover that the painful blisters I suffered while completing the Tóchar Phádraig have come back to haunt me. I continue, however, and eventually come out to a minor roadway beside a bungalow, which leads right for a short distance to join the main Dingle–Feohanagh road. With cars whizzing past and the pain beneath my toes getting worse, the clutches of middle age are now only too apparent. I suddenly feel that I've had enough and ring for rescue. My family are obviously having a worryingly good time without me but sportingly agree to come and pick me up. I dislike road walking, especially when shod in rigid mountain boots, and the last couple of kilometres seem interminable.

Rescue arrives as I head up the minor road that lies in the shadow of Brandon's bald head. Abandoning any semblance of a pilgrim tradition, I leave the last kilometre or so to Ballybrack car park for completion tomorrow. Gladly sitting in, I forsake the landscape that each day offers Ireland's last view of the setting sun and retreat gratefully to Dingle.

Author's note: In my eagerness to get to Kilmalkedar, I somehow walked passed the large circular stone fort which is conveniently located beside the pilgrim route at Caherdorgan East. This early medieval cashel is well worth the tiny diversion as it contains some fine examples of the clochán style dwellings that once characterised the Dingle Peninsula.

16

MOUNT BRANDON
SAINT'S ROAD | County Kerry

OVERVIEW Many resonances from the past are to be found on this relatively benign path that is well defined and simply heaves with spiritual symbolism. Walkers continuing on the extended route are rewarded with memorable views of the monumentally off-the-beaten-path monastic ruins at Fothair na Manach.

SUITABILITY An up-and-down outing on the Saint's Road to Mount Brandon's summit is straightforward navigationally as it follows a relatively clear path. Walkers choosing to do the full circuit north to join the Dingle Way should be fully equipped for a high-level outing and possess the required navigational skills. Be warned, however, that the descent into Fothair na Manach should be considered only by experienced walkers, who are not operating alone, are well used to steep ground and have the necessary fitness for the quad-burning re-ascent from the site. An added advantage would be a reassuring rope carried in a rucksack.

GETTING THERE Follow the harbour road to the west side of Dingle town. Go straight through the first roundabout and continue following the R459 and the signs for Brandon Creek. Eventually, a minor road to the right is signposted Mount Brandon and leads to Ballybrack (An Baile Breac) car park (Q434 095).

FINISH Ballybrack car park or Ballinknockane parking place (Q433 125).

TIME Allow 3 hours for the there-and-back walk on the Saint's Road to the summit, and 5 hours to complete the full circuit from Ballybrack to Ballinknockane. A further 2 hours should be added by those who descend, using extreme caution, the vertiginous Fothair Na Manach cliffs to visit the monastic ruins.

DISTANCE Saint's Road: 6km approx. Ballybrack to Ballyknockane: 9.5km. Circuit with Fothair Na Manach 10.5km.

HIGHEST ALTITUDE Brandon Mountain (924m).

MAP OSi map of Mount Brandon, 1:25,000.

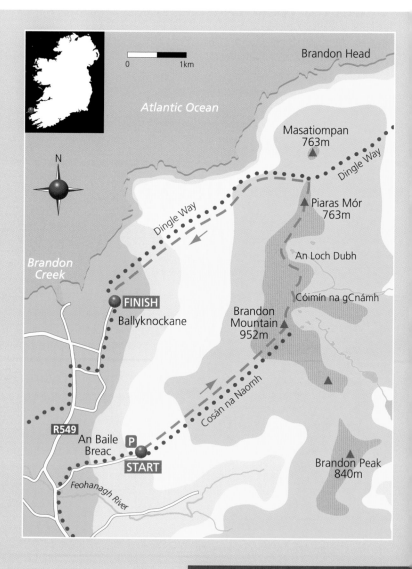

Brandon Head

Atlantic Ocean

Masatiompan
763m

Dingle Way

N

Dingle Way

Piaras Mór
763m

An Loch Dubh

Brandon
Creek

Cóimín na gCnámh

FINISH
Ballyknockane

Brandon
Mountain
952m

Cosán na Naomh

R549

An Baile
Breac

P

START

Brandon Peak
840m

Feohanagh River

Mount Brandon Saint's Road

These are days when Olympian efforts are made to eliminate even the slightest risk from our lives, with health and safety experts seeming determined to keep us all gibbering on until we're about 150. Children are no longer allowed walk to school, run in a playground or climb trees. Adults can't bring such bomb-making equipment as shampoo or baby food onto an aeroplane or buy more than two packets of paracetamol. Indeed, if Christopher Columbus lived today, he would hardly have reached the New World. An apparatchik would surely have appeared on the quayside just as he was about to set sail and listed at least twenty-nine reasons why the *Santa Maria* could not be licensed for a transatlantic passage.

So next morning, when I return to follow the benign Saint's Road to Brandon's summit, I discover that while the traditional pilgrimage extended to the summit of Brandon Mountain, the Cosán now officially ends at Ballybrack (An Baile Breac). My guidebook warns me that the mountain is hazardous, has steep cliffs, and is prone to sudden disorientating mists and points out that walkers proceed to the summit at their own risk.

Remembering, however, that early pilgrims rarely retreated from adversity, I square my shoulders and defiantly head up the mountain. The inveterate Irish traveller and polymath Robert Lloyd Praeger described Brandon as 'the finest mountain in Ireland', but from the west there is little hint of this. Indeed, it could more accurately be described as a typical Irish mountain: to the west, benign and gently angled; steep and ferocious to the east.

Mount Brandon from the west.

As I set out, I am immediately reminded of the spiritual significance of the mountain when, as at Faha on the east side, I pass another imposing Marian grotto that this time stands beside a picturesque mountain stream. There is also a poignant monument setting out the names of those who have walked the Cosán in hope of a cure for cancer. And as I head up the well-trodden path towards Brandon's summit, I can't help reflecting on the fickle grasp on life we all have and wondering if the Almighty responded to the self-sacrifice of those who had been dealt one of life's shortest straws.

Initially, I cross a bridge and continue uphill with a stream on my left to reach a gate. A little beyond this gate, I veer left from the main track and follow a line of white posts uphill over another bridge to reach the first of the fourteen Stations of the Cross that lead most of the way to the summit. The tradition of pilgrimage to Brandon Mountain apparently dates from early Christian times when the pagan deity Crom Dubh was reputedly evicted from his mountain stronghold by, you've guessed it, St Brendan. To this day, there remains a strong tradition of praying at each station on the way up.

Panoramic view of the Three Sisters taken from the Dingle Way.

I had never been up the Saint's Road before, but it proves pleasant and undemanding with a reassuringly well-defined path rising at a modest angle. Beyond an impressive standing stone, which marks the approximate halfway point, the path veers somewhat right and the going steepens and becomes a bit rocky but is never really demanding. On the approach to the summit, where the route is joined by a low wall from the south, I am pleased to discover that, for once, the top is cloud free.

Unlike my earlier ascent from the east side of the mountain, I am not alone on the top. The serenity has already been hijacked by an assembly of young people (from Kerry, to judge by their accents) who are already cheerfully buzzing around the cross like a swarm of animated bees. Immediately, I am roped in to take a photo of the summit-conquering group. Their leader then explains that St Brendan prayed here before setting out in a tiny boat to cross the storm-tossed Atlantic. On this voyage the saint thought he had discovered a new island. He only came to realise, to his consternation, that it was actually a giant sea monster when it began to move after he came ashore. He was undeterred by this initial setback, for the group leader, with admirable local patriotism, then confidently explains that there is little doubt that St Brendan subsequently went on to become, not only the first Kerry man, but also indeed the first European to reach America.

The group seem fascinated by all this and one lad points to the Blasket Islands and asks if the monster was as big as them. Another wants to know if St Brendan went as far as New York. Finally someone asks why the saint didn't simply stay on in America and convert the Indians. The leader could have pointed out here that it was almost a thousand years after St Brendan's voyage that Christopher Columbus mistakenly assumed he had arrived in India and referred to the Native Americans as Indians. Seemingly unprepared for this line of questioning he doesn't respond, however, and soon after the lecture ends and I find myself alone on the summit.

So far so simple, but now the question is: where to, next? It is, of course, possible to descend by my route of ascent, but I have other plans. So I swing left and descend a clearly defined track before traversing a broad crest above the brutal beauty of Coimín na gCnámh ('little coum of the bones'). Continuing now on a more defined ridge, I negotiate my way above the lonesome curl of water known as An Loch Dubh. The ridge broadens again, before descending to a broad col and then ascending to cross the substantial uprise to the bouldery head of Piaras Mór. Next I traverse the lesser eminence of Piaras Beg before dropping beside a fence

Looking down into Fothair Na Manach.

and passing to intercept the waymarked Dingle Way. Here, beneath the craggy south face of Masatiompan Mountain, which neatly bookends the northern extremity of the Brandon range, I come across yet another of Dingle's ubiquitous ogham stones. It bears a cross in a circle on one side while the inscription on the other side apparently reads, 'Ronan, the priest son of Comhgall.'

The route now follows the Dingle Way downhill, while I imbibe fully of the views, for beneath unfolds a magical meeting of sapphire sea, sky and shapely hills with the splendid Blasket Islands forming an impossibly pretty backdrop. And, to the right, is the unmistakable sandstone slit of Brandon Creek from where it is reputed that the first transatlantic voyage departed. What a very incongruous sight St Brendan and his followers must have made, setting off in their tiny animal-hide boat, without lifejackets, oilskins or navigational aids, to do what the 46,000-ton *Titanic* failed spectacularly to achieve – to cross the mighty North Atlantic. The likely route taken by St Brendan to the New World was memorably recreated in 1976, when Tim Severin made a weather-tortured voyage from Feohanagh to Newfoundland in a leather boat and thereby proved it was possible for a sixth-century monk to have reached North America.

Next, I head left towards huge cliffs and contour carefully along the edge. Then, the improbable patch of green I am searching for catches my eye. This is Fothair na Manach ('the green field of the monks', not noted on the Ordnance Survey map) – surely the remotest, most spectacular monastic site in Ireland. First-time visitors will immediately wonder how anyone, especially if shod only in medieval footwear, could possibly descend such monstrous cliffs to reach the ancient fields and clocháns, lying 400m below. And then, what fortitude gave these individuals the will to survive on a tiny patch of green several hundred feet above this wild, west Kerry shore.

The secret of safety on a mountain is to distinguish real hazards from just perceived danger. Careful investigation will show that descent is possible to the monastic ruins by a tortuous green ramp, which today is enveloped by snowdrifts of wild flowers. Don't be easily tempted, however, for this option carries real risk.

For most recreational walkers, discretion will prove the better part of valour and they will contour along the cliffs and then descend easily by a fence leading back to the Dingle Way. This is my plan of action after which I follow the Dingle Way downhill to the parking place at Ballinknockane.

17

ST FINBARR'S
PILGRIM PATH | County Cork

Drimoleague to Kealkill

OVERVIEW Undoubtedly Ireland's best laid out pilgrim route, it offers an excellent outing that is extremely well marked with walking arrows. A route with genuine charisma, it offers a huge variety of terrain and many memorable vistas. Despite the fact that it is one of the best, if not the best penitential trail in Ireland, it is not denoted as an official pilgrim path. Consequently, it is not waymarked with the familiar logo of a pilgrim with staff.

From the Top of the Rock you follow instead the yellow signage of the Sheep's Head Way through Castledonovan to the Mealagh Valley and then on to the tiny village of Kealkill. Here the route joins with the Beara–Breiffne Way, which leads you in fine style over the Sheehy Mountains to Gougane Barra.

At the time of writing, there was no official guidebook to the route. The guidebook to the *Sheep's Head Way Eastern Routes* is the most useful of what is available. The second half of the route from Carriganass Castle, Kealkill to Gougane Barra is described in reasonable detail. The first half of St Finbarr's Way is not described directly in the guidebook, but walks 6, 8 and 9 cover much of the route, although not always in the required direction.

SUITABILITY Expect a long day with a traverse of some high, isolated terrain. Route is well waymarked throughout. Never-theless, be equipped with good boots, gaiters, warm clothing and rain gear, and a map and compass just in case a waymarker is missing.

GETTING THERE From Cork city take the N71 to Bandon, then follow the R586 to Dunmanway and then the R588 to Drimoleague. The walk begins at Top of the Rock, 1km north of Drimoleague (W127 469) and ends at Carriganass Castle (W046 568) near Kealkill. There is no public transport from Kealkill to Drimoleague. You will need either to arrange a lift or organise a taxi.

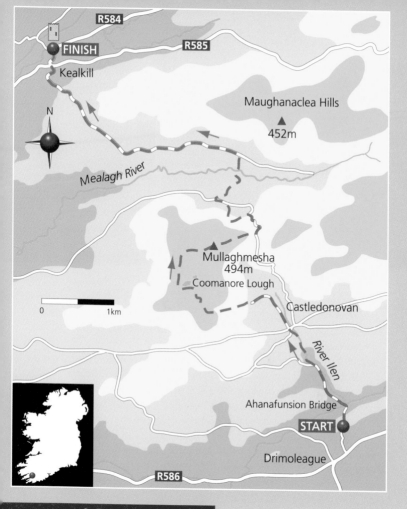

TIME 6 to 7 hours. **DISTANCE** 19km.

MAP OSi *Discovery Series* 85.

S t Finbarr's Pilgrim Path, west Cork – ever heard of it? Nor had I. Then, just as I was about to complete the Pilgrim Trails of Ireland, or so I thought, it sallied unexpectedly over the horizon. It seemed I had to check it out, but information proved elusive. The blurb from *Discover Ireland* informed me, with just the tiniest hint of hubris I thought, that 'this

Waymarker beyond Castledonovan.

newly-revived ancient pilgrim path is set to become the "Camino of West Cork". It then went on to say that the walk begins at the Top of the Rock, Drimoleague, where local tradition states that St Finbarr, who is now indisputably accepted as the patron saint of County Cork, chanced this way in the sixth century and admonished the people to return to Christ. Finbarr then went on his way to Gougane Barra, where he set up a small monastery before later moving on to become Bishop of Cork. His early journey from Drimoleague to Gougane Barra gave rise in succeeding years to a tradition of local people walking the 37km in pilgrimage, with the largest numbers doing this on 25 September, the saint's feast day. Beyond this biographical information, however, there was little detail on the actual route.

I phone Cork Tourist Office. No details of the route are available but they advise me to contact Fáilte Ireland. They helpfully provide me with what seems like information on every visitor attraction in Cork and Kerry, except, of course, St Finbarr's Pilgrim Path. Eventually, I excavate some information from the Internet concerning the second half of the trail beyond Kealkill, but the remainder continues to allude me. However, it transpires that the relevant guidebook is not, as I naively expect, entitled *St Finbarr's Pilgrim Path*, but instead is *The Sheep's Head Way Eastern Routes*.

It looks like I will have to go and find things out for myself. And so early one morning, equipped with a *Discovery Series* map that might or might not show some of St Finbarr's Way (it was actually hard to tell), I find myself heading towards Drimoleague and undiscovered west Cork. 'Undiscovered' for me, that is, since I knew relatively little about it from a walking point of view. A scramble up Hungry Hill and a couple ascents above Gougane Barra was about the extent of it.

Now the south-west of Ireland in good weather is a place so sublime that tourists continually wonder why they reside elsewhere. In misty overcast conditions, however, they are wont to express wonderment that local people have the fortitude to remain living there. And this is one of those mornings, for Drimoleague sits at the bottom of a great ocean of opaque drizzle.

My usual modus operandi in such circumstances is to retreat to a coffee shop and plan my next move, but there doesn't appear to be one. In Collin's Supermarket, the assistant has no idea where I would find details of St Finbarr's Way. So I purchase a takeout coffee, sit on a wall outside and gaze gloomily at the damp, empty streets and the Catholic church that dominates the hillside above.

In my own mind, I dub the place 'Grimoleague' and am smugly considering the astonishing cleverness of this when I notice an attractively decorated charity shop. I venture inside and am rewarded with an effusive welcome. The ladies behind the counter not only know of the pilgrim path, most have footed it all the way to Gougane Barra and they seem genuinely delighted that I am going to give it a go. I receive precise directions to the start point but they then warn me not to be overambitious, for I will need two long, hard days to complete it. One of the ladies lets me have her own copy of *The Sheep's Head Way Eastern Routes*. Soon after, I find myself ready for action at the Top of the Rock, reflecting that Drimoleague isn't so grim after all.

Then another problem presents itself. After all my efforts I now discover that the sophisticated-looking guidebook doesn't cover the first half of St Finbarr's Path either. It seems I am very much on a mystery tour of my own making. However, the well-constructed trail disappearing into the mist-laden valley seems almost to shout, 'walk me'. So I obediently follow the waymarkers down a steeply descending path where the route is denoted as both Slí Fhionn Barra and as the Sheep's Head Way. Later I discovered that the unique St Finbarr's Path markers appear on the posts all the way to Gougane Barra, alongside the Sheeps's Head Way sign plates. The mist begins clearing intermittently when I reach pretty Ahanafunsion Bridge, which allows me tantalising glimpses of the green and pleasant highlands above Castledonovan. A short distance on a quiet road is then followed by a traverse along the west bank of the River Ilen.

Here, a stately heron rises languidly before me as must often have happened in times past when the route served as a Mass path for the

Ancient tomb with capstone, located in woodland near the Mealagh River.

faithful. As I pass some photo-friendly cascades, the sun suddenly breaks through to dapple the hurrying waters. Emerging at Castledonovan, which is really just an intersection of roads, I follow the arrows left past the great ruined castle that served as the seat of the Donovan clan in the sixteenth century and which is now being consolidated and stabilised by the Irish Office of Public Works.

Hoping that I am still following the footsteps of Cork's patron saint, I head right and uphill through countryside where it is clear that Ireland's Celtic Tiger never left its calling card. This truly is undiscovered Ireland, replete with many old-style but scrupulously well-maintained farmhouses, painted in a pleasing vernacular white. Then it is through a gate along a firm green road, which, I later learn, was constructed to facilitate turf cutting in the upland bogs.

Passing an implausibly huge boulder that rises from the earth like the head of a subterranean monster, I continue through another gate. The path then takes me right and uphill to reveal an astonishing lake sitting like a giant reservoir above the surrounding bogs. Continuing upwards I cannot help wondering where the water in the lake comes from – there is nowhere for it to flow down from. Then there is also the mystery of how the surrounding bogland manages to retain it.

While mulling over this inexplicable enigma, the route conveys me to a high point near a telecommunications mast where a sign points ahead for the house of George the Sky. This appellation refers to George Mahony, a local hill farmer who earned the title by residing in a remarkably elevated abode on the hillside. Time is pressing on and I can't divert to investigate George's airy dwelling so instead I swing left and descend towards the staggeringly pretty Coomanore Lough. It is one of the most beguilingly attractive lakes I have ever seen and the impulse to linger awhile by its still waters is nigh irresistible.

Here, a feeling of serenity washes over me and for a while nothing else seems important. Then it occurs to me that this part of St Finbarr's

Way is almost exactly as I had imagined the perfect pilgrim trail to be – an evocative and serene upland path with stunning views of unspoiled countryside and an inescapable sense of going somewhere. If all pilgrim trails were like this, I feel right now that I could walk forever.

I push spryly ahead until the path disappears and waymarkers lead me around the western tip of the lake where a spur route goes left for Bantry. Now drenched in sunshine, I continue straight ahead though, through boggy terrain to reach the cairned summit of Mullaghmesha (494m). This is clearly a place to linger for on offer is a panoramic 360-degree view. Here my attention is especially captured by the great island-strewn expanse of Bantry Bay gleaming to the west.

Descending east along a broad ridge and then through a stand of commercial timber, I reach a paved road where the waymarkers point left and north. A further steep descent along a switchback byroad leads to another stile going left. First, the route lies along a firm forest roadway and then a forest path leading across a small stream to open mountainside. Here I am surprised to find the waymarkers rising again through very rough underfoot conditions. Soon, however, they begin descending again, crossing a couple of stiles to deposit me on the main road running along the southern edge of the Mealagh Valley. The route goes left and then almost immediately right and north along a tarmac road and later a firm gravel path to reach a turning circle. Here it plunges into a plantation and then brings me suddenly upon another link to the past in the form of an ancient burial tomb. Pausing awhile, I wonder who the personage lying here is and why they were of such importance that so many felt compelled to mark their passing by hauling the great capstone into place above their resting pace.

I have little time to reflect further on this, however, for immediately afterwards is a rapid transition from the ancient to the modern as I encounter a very expensive-looking steel bridge that ensures I remain dry and safe while crossing the River Mealagh. Next is another abrupt change of scenery as the path bisects a young broadleaved plantation to reach a public road. The next 4km or so along a fairly busy highway is not exactly the highlight of my day, but when the arrows go right, I am suddenly on a minor byroad descending to Kealkill with great sweeping vistas over Bantry Bay and the Beara Mountains beyond. Close to Kealkill a standing stone is signposted to the right, but I lack the energy to investigate. Instead, I push on wearily to Burke's shop on the main road from Bantry, where I enjoy an infusion of caffeine and a delectable muffin outside while waiting for a taxi to return me to Drimoleague.

18

ST FINBARR'S PILGRIM PATH
County Cork

Kealkill to Gougane Barra

OVERVIEW See p. 124.

SUITABILITY Strenuous outing that traverses a considerable amount of high, isolated terrain. Be aware that fog and cloud can descend quickly and make navigation problematic. Generally, the route is most suitable for experienced walkers equipped with good waterproof boots, gaiters, warm clothing and rain gear.

START/FINISH This leg of the walk begins at Carriganass Castle (W046 566), near Kealkill, and ends in the valley of Gougane Barra (W094 662). There is no public transport from Gougane Barra to Kealkill. You will need either to arrange a lift or organise a taxi.

FOOD Available at Drimoleague, Kealkill and Gougane Barra.

TIME 6 to 7 hours. **DISTANCE** 19km.

HIGHEST ALTITUDE Lough Fadda (526m).

MAP OSi *Discovery Series* 85.

'Were you off for a bit of a stroll?' The questioner is a tall man with high cheekbones and an engaging mixture of accents that, I guess, makes him an Englishman in Ireland, but universally regarded as Irish when in England. It is a week after my long walk to Kealkill and I am back in west Cork to complete the final leg of St Finbarr's Pilgrim Way.

Arriving early in tiny Kealkill on the day before my walk, I decide to try and get a proper fix on the route since I have already noted that the first section is almost entirely on road. So I drive past Carriganass Castle and then follow the signs for Gougane Barra along what is known locally as the Maugha Road. On the way, Maughanasilly standing stones, signposted to the right, capture my curiosity enough for a visit. And my effort is well rewarded, for its five huge upright boulders are bathed in

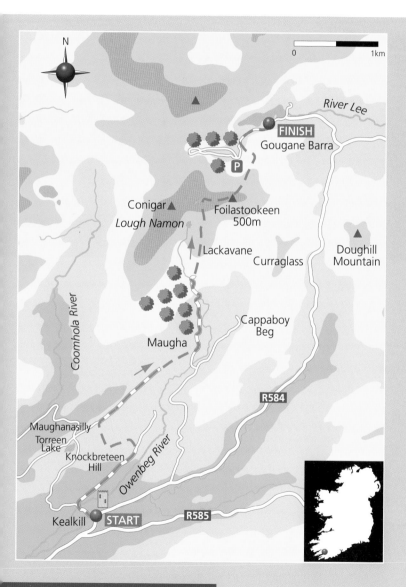

St Finbarr's Pilgrim Path

Maughanasilly standing stones.

an evocatively surreal glow of evening light. And here, the veil of time lifts briefly and I feel just a little in touch with the prehistoric past.

Next, it is onwards past lonesome Torreen Lake until, at the end of the road, a gate bearing a comforting welcome sign bars my wheels. Now, on foot, I pass a quaint house with a partly thatched roof and then poke around for a bit to clear my mind about the exact direction of tomorrow's route. And it is on my way back that I encounter Mike as he unhurriedly feeds titbits to a mule and a donkey. In answer to his question, I tell him I am not walking today, but am intent on completing the pilgrim route over the hills to Gougane Barra.

In the best Irish tradition we then 'get into chat' and he tells me that he has lived in Ireland for forty years. It was 1972 when he came to west Cork with his girlfriend after leaving Oxford University. 'It was a hard life in those days but we loved it', he tells me, with a wistful twinkle of remembrance in his eyes. 'Our only transport was a donkey and cart.' Then he recalls, with rich vivacity, battling through snowdrifts while using this form of transport to fetch supplies from the village.

He is exceptionally well versed in the folklore and traditions of the area and speaks knowledgeably of O'Sullivan Beare and his great forced march north through the area in the seventeenth century. Vividly he recalls seeing groups of pilgrims passing by on their way from Drimoleague to Gougane Barra for many years and he also knows much about early twentieth-century freedom fighter Tom Barry, who operated a successful insurgency in west Cork. Then he smiles and says how ironic it is that it now falls on an Englishman to recount to an Irishman the stories passed to him by previous generations of people from the surrounding hills.

Before we part, he tells me I will be following in exalted company on tomorrow's walk. Apparently no less a personage than the British ambassador led about twenty walkers over the hills to Gougane Barra some time previously, with the group enjoying a huge picnic high on the hillsides above us. And does Mike mind so many walkers literally passing outside his doorstep? 'At my age, why should I mind? The place will be here after me,' is his insightful reply.

Next morning, I am back at Carriganass Castle, but this time on foot and ready to complete my pilgrimage to Gougane Barra. Immediately taking the road left over the Owenbeg River, I then go right along a shaded byroad that gradually rises into the hill country. After about thirty minutes of pleasant but unspectacular walking, I leave the tarmac by a stile on the left and follow the arrows along a forest track which then ascends sharply to a fence bisecting the sawtooth eminence of Knockbreteen

St Finbarr's Oratory at Gougane Barra. (Paula Elmore)

Hill. Memorable views abound in every direction and I easily pick out Knockboy (County Cork's highest hill, 706m) to the north-west and the unmistakable outline of Hungry Hill adorning the south-western skyline.

Tagging the fence left leads me to a steep, undulating and marshy firebreak that descends directly to a stile on what I hope is the Maugha Road. It is, for the signs point reassuringly right towards Gougane Barra. I follow these for about 2km while thinking what a lonely and isolated but also sensational place this would be to live. When I reach the 'gateway of the welcomes' encountered yesterday there is no sign of Mike. So I dutifully follow the waymarkers through what appears like a sawmill and then out onto open heathland on a rough track.

Eventually, the comforting track is no more and immediately I begin sinking into boot-kidnapping wetlands. I used to think trees couldn't survive in a marsh, but apparently they can, for when I enter woodland the going still remains wet and trying. It is only for a short distance though, and then I am glad to place my boots firmly on the upper reaches of Lackavane road. Following the fence left leads me to a steep, undulating and marshy firebreak that descends directly to a stile on what I hope is the Maugha Road. About twenty minutes later, having crossed a bridge over the Owenbeg River, I reach the end of the road. Here, it is up an avenue, passing by an incongruously located herd of Scottish Highland cattle, before traversing a rough field to reach a lane at the back of a blue painted farmhouse.

Initially, a rather strenuous climb up the firm, stony lane leads to Lackavane Ridge. At the end of the track, waymarkers lead across open mountain. Then they join a fence which disappears left over the crest of the hill while, to the west, squadrons of shower clouds are sweeping in ominously from Kerry. It is not a particularly taxing ascent as I follow the fence upwards so I have the energy to enjoy views over Lough Namon which appears serenely on the left as I gain height.

Then a shower locks onto me with the unerring accuracy of a guided missile and I become aware of a piercing chill as the path undulates and then crosses a stile between two lakes. Just beyond, the rain eases a bit and suddenly I come upon awe-inspiring views over the great Coomrua cliffs to St Finbarr's Oratory and the impossibly beautiful and tranquil lake at Gougane Barra. It is a captivating vista. Despite the cold and spitting rain, I spent an inordinate amount of time gazing as though hypnotised at the sublime views, as previous pilgrims must, almost universally, have been moved to do. Eventually, I am reluctantly forced to tear myself away and follow a fence to the right that gently rises to the fine viewing point of Foilastookeen (500m). From here I can just make out the location of a huge gully known locally as Poll a few hundred metres to my left.

Immediately the story of an almost miraculous escape down this great cleft bubbles into my consciousness. In June 1921, the IRA's West Cork Flying Column of over a hundred men retreated up the Borlin Valley towards the Cork/Kerry border. They were commanded by the charismatic Tom Barry, who had recently rendered Cork virtually ungovernable with a successful terror campaign against Crown forces. In hot pursuit were thousands of British troops who had been deployed to west Cork for the sole purpose of eliminating him, while more soldiers blocked his escape route to Kerry. The position seemed hopeless until Barry did the unexpected. Having apparently collected every piece of rope in the valley, he moved his men under cover of darkness out onto the mountains and headed towards Gougane Barra. If this sanctuary could be reached, he knew he would be safely outside the British blockade on the Pass of Keimaneigh.

Well I recall reading Barry's gripping account from his book, *Guerrilla Days in Ireland,* of a nightmarish march in thick darkness, often sinking knee-deep in boggy ground. Eventually the column reached the top of Poll, a steep, rocky defile that narrows to an unstable gully but offered an escape route to Gougane Barra. Guided by local man Monty Cronin, the volunteers slithered down, supported by their rifles and ropes. An hour later 'bruised and wrenched', but without other injury, they reached the valley and a short time later were enjoying the hospitality of Cronin's Hotel. Soon after, British forces abandoned the blockade having realised they had been outwitted once again.

Glad that I am not required to descend Poll, I instead begin carefully traversing the slippery rocks below the summit. I wonder what Barry, who fought ' the mother of all battles' to drive the British out of west Cork, would now make of the ironic fact that almost every second person I had encountered spoke with an English accent. Like many questions arising on my pilgrim journey, I have no way of knowing but something tells me he would have been OK with these resolutely non-establishment migrants.

Anyway, I must now concentrate on tracking the invaluable yellow markers and paint splashes of the Beara–Breiffne Way. These descend steeply enough at first but then more benignly to reach a stile at the corner of a wood. Crossing this, I come upon a rough track which then dog-legs down past some farm buildings. Eventually it emerges on the floor of the valley beside an unusual-looking thatched toilet block. The sign outside states – and I kid you not – that this edifice won an award as Ireland's 'Toilet of the Year'. Unfortunately, there is no way to establish what special features qualified it for this honour as it is now late and the building has been locked for the night.

Then I ramble up the valley and complete my pilgrim odyssey with a visit to St Finbarr's Oratory, a dreamily located small church built in the late nineteenth century on an island in Gougane Barra lake. This mesmerisingly attractive lake is also the source of the River Lee, and close to where the sixth-century monastery of St Finbarr was originally located. Continuing on towards Cronin's Hotel and the welcome promise of food, I reflect upon the timeless allure and immutable rustic charm of the landscape around me. When the carrot of cash from mass tourism is dangled temptingly, even the most sublime locations tend to surrender their most cherished values immediately. Not so Gougane Barra, however, which continues staunchly true to its ageless appeal and remains now much as it was in the time when Tom Barry and his flying column dropped in from the hills above, as unexpected but effusively welcomed visitors.

And later in the snug, old-world surroundings of Cronin's Bar, I conclude that I must now revise my earlier rather dismissive opinions of the route I have just completed. The realisation has dawned compellingly that it actually required little in the way of hubris to describe the magnificent St Finbarr's Pilgrim Way as 'the Camino of West Cork'.

19

CNOC NA dTOBAR | County Kerry

OVERVIEW Myth-laden mountain with a pilgrim tradition reaching back to pagan times; its summit offers expansive vistas over virtually the entire south-west of Ireland. The serpentine pilgrim path leads from just above sea level to an enchanting summit with new vistas opening up with almost every step.

SUITABILITY This is a there-and-back trail that is very clearly marked, starting gently and becoming more strenuous near the summit. It leads to a high summit (690m) that can be windy and cold, so be equipped with suitable clothing, footwear and, perhaps, walking poles, which can be particularly useful on the descent. Please also note that those wishing to satisfy the requirements for the Irish pilgrim passport need only climb to the eleventh station.

GETTING THERE Turn off the N70/Ring of Kerry road, to cross the bridge in Cahersiveen and take the first right and second left. Pass St Fursey's Well. Park at the car park on the right where all-day parking costs (at the time of writing) €3.00.

TIME 3.5 hours.

DISTANCE 6 km to the 11th station, 9 km to the summit.

HIGHEST ALTITUDE 690m.

MAP OSi *Discovery Series* 83.

The Ring of Kerry delivers a heady cocktail of compelling experiences – towering mountains, secluded beaches, shed-loads of heritage and even a dark-sky reserve. A tourism Mecca for generations, it still manages to retain a bank of intriguing secrets. One of the great pleasures I have found is that the Ring keeps on giving me the joy of discovery – such

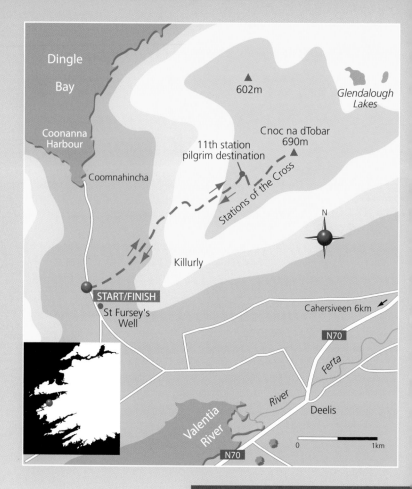

Dingle
Bay

602m

Glendalough
Lakes

Coonanna
Harbour

Cnoc na dTobar
690m

11th station
pilgrim destination

Coomnahincha

Stations of the Cross

N

Killurly

START/FINISH

Cahersiveen 6km

St Fursey's
Well

N70

Ferta

River

Deelis

Valentia
River

N70

0   1km

Cnoc na dTobar

as going a little off the main drag to get up close and personal with one of its sequestered gems, like Cnoc na dTobar (Mountain of Wells).

Largely untouched by modernity, this mythical place of pagan assemblies and Lughnasa overindulgences has, until recently, maintained a dignified indifference to the hire cars and coaches scuttling past its muscular ramparts as they circuit the Ring of Kerry. Increased footfall came when it was recognised, in 2014, as one of Ireland's penitential mountains. Now, I have come to join a group setting out to complete the first Irish pilgrim journey of its kind, while also checking the local claim that here is Ireland's most breathtaking vista.

Pilgrim walkers making their way towards the summit of Cnoc na dTobar.

Under the knowledgeable leadership of local man Johnny Keating, who hails from the nearby townland of Foilmore, we set out, forty-seven strong and beneath a cloud-flecked sky, on the first steps in a 125km pilgrim journey designated by the new Irish pilgrim passport. Beginning from the traditional start point for Cnoc na dTobar lying near St Fursey's Holy Well, which reputedly offers a cure for blindness, we pursue the convenient handrail provided by fourteen Stations of the Cross, marking the ancient summit trail. Built in the nineteenth century by Canon Brosnan, a larger-than-life parish priest from Castleisland in north Kerry who also constructed the Daniel O'Connell Memorial Church in nearby Cahersiveen, the crosses were recently supplemented with poles and yellow markers by enthusiastic local community activist, Cormac Dineen.

Initially the trail is benign, if a little tedious underfoot, as it meanders a little left in an apparent effort to find the line of least resistance while crackingly good coastal views unfold south-west over Coonanna Harbour, Dingle Bay and twin-topped Killelan Mountain. Modern pilgrimage is, of course, a quest for slowness and so there is plenty of time for Johnny to provide nuggets of information about the surrounding landscape. First, he informs us that the mountain has had a site of devotion to St Fursey since early Christian times, when the saint was reputedly cured of blindness at the well that now bears his name. Then he draws on a lifetime of local knowledge to dismiss the squall that appears to threaten us from the ocean to the west as 'not the slightest problem in the world; you see, the wind today is from the east'.

Later, he points directly to the birthplaces of the two famous local members of the O'Connell clan: Daniel and Mick. Barrister Daniel was born to a dispossessed Catholic family residing in a relatively humble abode at Carhan, the ruins of which still remain just outside the town of Cahersiveen. He was raised by his wealthy, childless uncle, Maurice 'Hunting Cap' O'Connell, at Derrynane House, which lies further south along the Ring of Kerry, and went on to become known as Ireland's Liberator, when he won the right for Catholics to enter parliament. Football legend Mick hailed from Valentia Island, which is laid out below Cnoc na dTobar like a giant ship moored neatly to the Kerry coastline. Overcoming the sporting handicap of living on an island, he went on to become regarded as the greatest exponent of Gaelic football.

Valentia Island's other claim to fame is that it was once the epicentre of world communication. An accident of geography made this the optimum place from which to send the first transatlantic electronic message, which was transmitted in 1866. The location was later considered so crucial that it was heavily fortified by British soldiers during the First World War. This did not prevent a coded message being forwarded by local nationalists in 1916, informing Irish republicans in New York that the Easter Rising had begun in Dublin.

Halfway up, Cnoc na dTobar reasserts itself just a little. The going steepens but never becomes really challenging as the path weaves its way eccentrically upwards towards the mountain's sinuous south-west ridge. It is only necessary to reach the eleventh station in order to fulfil the requirements for obtaining a passport stamp, but as one, every man and woman in our group continues onwards towards the summit.

So far so pleasant, but I still ponder what has drawn multitudes to pant up this mountainside since time unrecorded. The mountain answers on gaining Cnoc na dTobar's sinuous south ridge. A majestic vista radiates south-west over the multiple bays and inlets around Cahersiveen and Valentia, as the ocean spectacularly drowns the Kerry land mass. Floating in deep blue beyond is Ireland's last stand against the Atlantic – the dreamy Skellig rocks, which, Johnny now tells us proudly, have been designated a World Heritage Site. Dursey Island tugs the eye southwards as it clings like a droplet to the fingernail of Beara while further along the ridge lies a magical prospect: the unmistakeable outline of Carrauntoohil – Ireland's highest peak at 1,040m – amid the angular MacGillycuddy's Reeks.

The Canon's Cross at the summit of Cnoc na dTobar.

An imposing Celtic cross on the summit plateau, which is known locally as the Canon's Cross, has recently been refurbished. Clearly, the site was well chosen, for it offers arresting views to Kerry's other sacred mountain: Mount Brandon. The extensive mountaintop was also selected to host the singing, dancing, athletic contests and merrymaking associated with the ancient festival of Lughnasa. Otherwise, it is unspectacular, for the reward hereabouts lies with distance.

The highest point lies a little further on and offers us an entrancing panorama over the mountains of Dingle to the surreal outline of the Blasket Islands. Lording it over the surrounding uplands, it offers the perfect 360-degree vista, not just beautiful but hauntingly visceral as well. For a time everyone stands silent and intoxicated by the magic beneath our feet. To conceive of a comparable Irish mountaintop spectacle is difficult – perhaps Mount Brandon, perhaps Slieve Carr, perhaps Errigal.

From here we could follow the ridge, above the postcard-perfect Glendalough lakes, before descending to Kells Bay on the north side of the mountain after about 4½ hours' walking. Instead we retrace our steps, with general unanimity emerging that the four remaining pilgrim

Coonanna Harbour seen from the slopes of Cnoc na dTobar.

paths required by our passport journey have a hard act to follow if they are to exceed the memories that Cnoc na dTobar has bestowed today. Having my pilgrim passport stamped that evening in the Old Barracks in Cahersiveen, one fact seems indisputable – Cnoc na dTobar is for a clear day when the extravagant vista will remain forever stamped in the imaginings of all who aspire to its magical summit.

20

SKELLIG MICHAEL | County Kerry

OVERVIEW Despite the requirements of health and safety, this is still one of the most memorable touristic experiences in Ireland. Unlike Croagh Patrick and Lough Derg, however, Skellig Michael has retained very little of its original spirituality, with few visitors now seeking a deep religious experience. These days it perhaps best fits into the category of early Christian experiential tourism.

SUITABILITY In the uncompromising penitential tradition there are no toilets or shelter on the island. If you have already climbed a mountain such as Croagh Patrick or Slieve League you are unlikely to have any trouble on Skellig Michael. Nevertheless, the 600-plus steps may not be suitable for the seriously unfit or for those who suffer from vertigo.

GETTING THERE Each year licences are granted to south Kerry boat owners who each run single daily trips to Skellig Michael between April and October, weather permitting. Most of these day trips depart from Portmagee or Ballinskelligs and the fare at the time of writing was generally €50, with no reduction for children. Most of the boat owners supply oilskins to protect against sea spray during the crossing. Visitors are usually allowed a little over 2 hours on the island.

It is best to book a place on the boats in advance and then to check with the boat owner on the day prior to sailing to make sure that boats are likely to run the next morning. The most sheltered seats on the majority of boats are the ones facing backwards from behind the wheelhouse.

EQUIPMENT Visitors to Skellig Michael need to wrap up well, have waterproofs in case it rains and carry their own lunch. A walking stick may be useful for some parts of the descent from the monastery.

TIME The round trip including sea crossing takes 4.5 to 5 hours.

MAP OSi *Discovery Series* 84, but the map in this book is more useful.

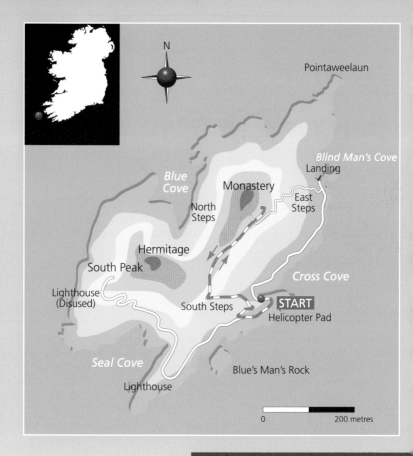

Skellig Michael

D o you believe, like I do, that tourism has become over-contrived – all sugar-coated activities, second-hand experiences and warnings about not touching the exhibits or falling down the escalator? Well, the good news is that experiential tourism has become the latest buzzword within the industry, with travellers facilitated to leave the visitor cocoon and sample authentic experiences. One of the best ways to do this is by traversing the open ocean in an uncovered boat through great rolling swells and stinging salt spray, but health and safety experts have now ensured that this is an increasingly rare experience. Thankfully, however, the wind-tortured, 12km open boat journey from south Kerry to Skellig Michael survives and forms the final, and for me, the most eagerly anticipated destination of my pilgrim odyssey.

Boats landing at Skellig Michael. (Valerie O'Sullivan)

Having been there before, but almost two decades ago, I am now interested to see if the arrival of mass tourism to Ireland and the shifting sands of time have impacted on this hauntingly memorable experience. And to ensure this, I have to get there before the boats to Skellig are tied up for the winter.

From Killarney to Waterville I go, not by way of the main Ring of Kerry road, but to add a little variety I drive instead through the spine of the Iveragh Peninsula. And then in the gentle brushstrokes of the soft evening light, lavish autumn hues embellish one of Ireland's most unforgettable landscapes – a sensational muddle of wild mountains plunging to a lonesome lake-bejewelled valley. Dusk has descended when, with a glorious harvest moon as my guide, I ascend the Ballaghisheen Pass and then traverse the almost deafeningly silent and delightfully darkened Kerry outback to reach the south coast.

Waterville isn't postcard pretty but it is undeniably an appealing place for people to relax and tonight it is humming. The – believe it or not – Charlie Chaplin Festival is in full swing and paying unrestrained homage to a cinema superstar who made this south Kerry village his holiday home for many years. Now I realise that Charlie was to blame for the fact that, earlier in the week, overnight accommodation proved so elusive.

I get a booking at the Waterville Lake Hotel, known – and signposted – locally as Club Med. Everyone, it seems is at the Chaplin Festival, because, the receptionist apart, there isn't another soul in the place as I rattle off along a darkened corridor to my room.

Next morning I rise with bright sunshine streaming through the curtains and one of the most arresting views you could ever see from a hotel bedroom. From below my private balcony, a lake unfurls its aquamarine carpet towards a line of austere hills misting to the distance.

Later when I enquire about breakfast the receptionist says, 'ah yes, that's in the Waterville Bay Hotel.' Then, noting my bewildered look, she adds comfortingly, 'It's less then a mile away in the village.' Driving to breakfast? I know that in Las Vegas you are generally obliged to head through the seductive charms of the hotel casino to get your cornflakes, but a 'drive-in breakfast' is a new one for me.

In Waterville my full Irish is indeed a hearty one and is enlivened by some impromptu poetic entertainment from a local man (why do all Kerry men seem so effortlessly poetic?), who is clearly one of last night's revellers from the Charlie-fest.

Afterwards, with the first infusion of autumn in the air, I head east along the coast road to Portmagee and my 10 a.m. appointment with a boat to Skellig Michael. Robert Lloyd Praeger describes the Skellig Islands as 'two rocks … of lovely outline, towering like cathedrals. The larger, the Great Skellig, rises 714 feet and clinging to the cliffs like swallows' nests are the huddled houses of anchorites of olden days.' What Praeger refers to as 'clinging to the cliffs' is the early Christian monastery, which is reputed to have been founded in the sixth century by St Fionain. The monastery is believed to have survived against astronomical odds until the twelfth century when it was abandoned, with the monks moving to Ballinskelligs during a period of Church reform. Skellig Michael then became yet another Irish place of pilgrimage and penance in the medieval period, with pilgrims coming from as far away as Europe to pray on this windswept rock that, until a few hundred years ago, sat perilously on the very edge of the explored world.

As I reach Portmagee, the weather forecast comes on the car radio with the following ominous message: 'Deepening depression of 996 hectopascals centred 400 miles west of Valentia drifts steadily eastwards. It and its associated frontal system will cross the south-west coast of Ireland later today and early tonight.' An incoming storm! Let's hope we can get back to the mainland before it breaks.

At the quayside, I note that my comfortably attired fellow travellers seem better acquainted with Gucci and Calvin Klein than sackcloth

Pilgrim steps on Skellig Michael.

View looking down the east steps on Skellig Michael leading to the alternative landing place at Blind Man's Cove.

and ashes. Only twelve are allowed in each boat and we are a motley collection of Irish and English, along with a couple of beardy Austrian men – who admit that this is their first open ocean adventure –and a matey, baseball-capped American. All are, I guess, not so much seeking a redemptive exercise as an enhanced holiday experience.

Immediately it becomes obvious that we have succeeded in escaping the cotton-wool clutches of the twenty-first century when we climb down the vertical steel ladder to board the bobbing boat. Afterwards, the crossing is gloriously unsanitised as we slice through a spiritedly uncooperative ocean. Predictably, the American, who has already informed us that he is over for a much-hyped Notre Dame against Navy football game in Dublin, soon announces that he is 'just lovin' this vacation in the Emerald Isle'. Then apparently failing to recollect the reason for his Irish visit, he adds the proviso that Dublin 'isn't bad, but it's just far too packed with vacationers.'

Eventually, we are all forced to cower in oilskins as waves from the huge swells break over us. One of the travellers from landlocked Austria exclaims, 'der Ozean ist so gross', while our American friend pronounces the huge swells around us as 'like, totally awesome'. And then the boat seems to almost leap clear of the ocean before coming down with a resounding crack while water sloshes around our feet. Like passengers on a turbulent aircraft seeking reassurance from the flight attendant, all eyes immediately turn towards our skipper. We then take comfort from the fact that he seems monumentally unconcerned by it all and continues chatting languidly on his phone.

As we approach Little Skellig, the sea moderates and canny gannets now follow hungrily in our slipstream. And then lo – there it is, straight ahead: the perfectly symmetrical shark-tooth island that somehow seems sedately indifferent to the puny inroads of 21st-century tourism. An hour out from the mainland, we fetch up at the Skellig Michael quayside where a nimble step is required to reach the island. The monastic ruins towering above us seem almost to knock on heaven's door.

Immediately, we are all ordered into a circle for our compulsory health and safety lecture, which makes me wonder what the early monks would have made of all this. Like primary school children on an outing, we are told by not to rush, to watch where we are putting our feet, to keep to the inside of the path and to stop walking when taking photographs. And then looking rather pointedly at me, I thought, the safety officer instructs us to tie up our shoelaces.

Having obediently secured our laces and agreed that we understand the instructions, we are released. Now it is a question of testing the body but elevating the spirit on the 600 penitentially steep steps. Since my

Beehive huts with Little Skellig in the background.

last visit, there has been a noticeable increase in the number of safety barriers and chains but these interventions, while perhaps necessary, become fewer as we ascend. A grassy col about halfway up, which is known Christ's Saddle, is where most visitors stop to draw breath and take in the splendid views.

Here our American acquaintance breathlessly pronounces Skellig Michael as 'just swell' but then expresses deep puzzlement as to why the early men of God were inconsiderate enough to choose almost the highest point of the island for their monastery. 'Why didn't they just build it here?' he asks of nobody in particular as he gazes at the unappetisingly steep staircase rising ahead. 'It would have made it so much easier and safer for everyone and more comfortable in a storm,' he huffs. Privately I think that early Christian monks were not noted for their dedication to creature comforts.

The most noticeable change from my previous visit is that most of the island is now closed to visitors. Heretofore, you could ramble as you fancied. Impetuously perhaps, I had taken advantage of this by ascending the South Peak to view the stunning hermitage – an even more inaccessible place of prayer clinging precariously to rocky ledges

200m above the ocean. In the intervening years the hermitage has been restored and consolidated amid controversy, with some critics pointing out that what has happened actually amounts to a modern rebuilding.

A guide is explaining to a group of Dutch visitors that not only did the early monks climb up and down the South Peak on a regular basis, they also managed to build the hermitage. Apparently, unaware of the irony, he then explains that the area is too steep and dangerous to allow visitors access to the area and this is why the South Peak has now been fenced off. Here, I can't help pondering that the selfsame 'steep and dangerous' argument could be used to close off Carrauntoohil and many other vertiginous mountains.

Clearly, what we are doing today is, by modern standards, a tough visitor experience not suitable for everyone. It is made more palatable, however, by powerful steel boats and safety interventions on the upward climb. The early inhabitants of Skellig Michael had, by comparison, a much more delicate grasp on life. Obliged to brave these monstrous seas in their animal-hide currachs, they would have landed by somehow beaching these tiny boats on the unforgiving rocks ringing the island. Climbing to the monastery would then have been accomplished without the aid of security chains and safety fences.

Now Murphy's Law suggests that if something can go wrong, sooner or later, it will. Continuing to ascend, I speculate about the fate of these early monks. It seems inconceivable that some were not lost in storms on the treacherous crossing from the mainland. Did others fall from the unforgiving cliffs as some modern visitors have also done? Were they ever cut off for so long that they ran short of food? I guess we will never know the answer to these questions but one thing is certain, these early Irish men of piety must have been teak tough and enormously religiously motivated to survive this brutally unforgiving environment.

When we arrive at the monastic site, the buildings seem ingeniously shoehorned into the tiny area, but they also look resolutely functional and minimalist. The exquisite ornamentation of the Tara Brooch, the Ardagh Chalice or the Cross of the Scriptures was never going to be created in a place where mere survival was the daily imperative. The surprise is not so much that this monastery is not very large and ornate and did not create something sublimely beautiful like the Book of Kells, but that it managed to come into existence at all and then for six centuries triumphed over huge adversity.

Greetings are extended to the group by Catherine who tells us she is from Wexford and is a guide on the island during the summer months. She tells us that relatively little has been recorded about the

Skellig monastery, which immediately makes me guess that the monks were too busy fishing for supper to find time for keeping a diary.

Archaeological evidence, she tells us, suggests that the inhabitants of the monastery lived on fish, eggs, a small vegetable garden they had created, and that they might have maintained a few domestic animals as well. Rain was the only source of water and was collected in cleverly designed cisterns. So vividly does she describe life on the island, or perhaps more accurately 'the rock', that we don't need to stretch our imaginations far to understand the brutal work ethic required to survive on this storm-lashed pinnacle and to marvel at the simple faith that sustained these early Christian monks amidst the harshness of the Atlantic Ocean. Finally, she advises us to be careful on the way down and hopes we will be back safely on the mainland before the weather deteriorates. This comment immediately evokes much fretful examining of the sky and sends some visitors scurrying immediately down the steps towards the boats.

I hang around, however, and get into chat with Catherine who tells me she spends two weeks on the island and then has one week on shore leave. Having now observed that the sun already has a golden ring – a sign of an approaching storm – I ask what it is like when a full-on Atlantic gale pounds the island. 'It can get pretty bad, all right', she tells me. 'Sometimes we have to crawl around on our hands and knees, but you get used to it,' she adds. And how does she cope when cut off from the mainland? Unexpectedly, she replies, 'Oh, I love it. It's when I really have time to myself. I take photographs; I write a little; I play music. It's great.' And remembering that this is Sunday, I enquire when she expects the next boat to reach the island. 'Wednesday I guess, although it could be Thursday or maybe Friday.'

All too soon it is time to say farewell to Catherine and head back down the steps to the quayside to rejoin our boat. On the return journey, we heave to near Little Skellig for a photo-op of the huge colony of garrulous gannets inhabiting the island, where no landings are allowed. Then it's full speed ahead for Portmagee.

Postscript

As I disembark from the boat at Portmagee, I feel a certain sense of elation. I have completed my journey along the pilgrim paths of Ireland, which began over four months ago in Belfast. Along the way, some of the routes have staunchly retained much of their original redemptive element, such as the Tóchar Phádraig, Lough Derg and the Cosán na Naomh where I hardly encountered another soul. Others such as Skellig Michael, Slieve League and the route up Croagh Patrick from Murrisk have all been colonised by mass tourism, but still managed to maintain much of their original mysticism.

And I have enjoyed all of the pilgrim paths, if only for the perceptible feeling of walking arm in arm with the ghosts of the past. There was also the addictive sense of completion that comes with the now rare experience of walking with a destination in mind. Marvelling at the great variety of landscapes they offer, I have continually wondered how all the pilgrim paths have been packed neatly into such a small country. Twenty-first-century Ireland has in many ways rejected the practice of formal religion, yet there can be little doubt that a deep and restless yearning for spiritual fulfilment continues to exist. There were the young people at Lough Derg queuing on a holiday weekend for the world's toughest pilgrimage; the grossly unfit pilgrims battling prayerfully up Croagh Patrick; the cancer victims walking the Cósan na Naomh and the touching idealism of the couple renewing their vows at Kilmalkeder.

At a quayside pub, I order a coffee and gaze across the peaceful waters to the green hills of Valentia Island. The sky is darkening to the west as I watch the last Skellig boat of the day make its languid way home. It is often said that the most worthwhile experiences in life come free of charge and it seems to me that the captivating allure of a pilgrim journey is that it lies well beyond the reach and influence of wealth and acts as a stark reminder that everything we have ultimately comes to us on loan. Consciously, we abandon the world of branded convenience and motorised travel in favour of the metronomic rhythms and greatly simplified existence that comes with walking a redemptive trail. Rich or poor, saint or sinner, sophisticate or not, are all equally likely to suffer overpowering fatigue, blister badly or even break an ankle while single-mindedly focusing on the simple goal of reaching the day's objective.

Clearly, I have now reached mine for I have just been to the edge of what was once the known world. It is the end of summer and the time has come to step back into the world of work, college and domesticity.

The wanderer in me would like to stumble on, of course, finding new places for more profound challenges by, perhaps, following in the wake of Columba to Scotland, Brendan to Greenland or the Slieve League monks to Iceland. And, indeed, there is something addictive and strangely comforting about the stoical simplicity of roving ancient pilgrim paths. They may not have exactly moved me to a life of atonement and service but I have, nevertheless, been drawn in by an indefinable magic and sense of purpose that makes one part of me want to go on and on.

But spirituality, scenery and ghosts of the past aside, I have found completing my journey to be genuinely hard, unforgiving work. I have ascended over 4,000m and I have also completed about 190km of pilgrim paths, which I suppose is not exactly like walking the Appalachian Trail. Certainly, it is inconsequential compared with the privations endured by the early Irish Christian monks, known as the Peregrini, who chose to leave the security of their monasteries and travel around Europe bringing the gospel to new believers, shining a light in the Dark Ages.

Nevertheless, the effort has left me feeling weary and somewhat footsore, while massively awestruck by the unswerving commitment of Ireland's early Christian missionaries. Along the way I have become only too aware of my own frailties and of not really having what it takes for the true redemptive experience. I am tired of poring over maps, searching for missing waymarkers, getting soaked by Ireland's worst summer for a century, and having aching feet while rattling around hotel rooms on my own. Our early saints were undoubtedly much hardier individuals. Apparently lacking any form of self-doubt, they renounced all the comforting securities of home, family and familiar landscapes to follow the beckoning hand of destiny over a wholly unknown horizon. Clearly, they believed that true fulfilment came not in the pursuit of wealth and pleasure, but with the act of serving. To this end, they were unquestionably resolute and self-sacrificing and would almost certainly, I imagine, have regarded me as a sinner in urgent need of salvation.

Finishing my coffee, I throw my rucksack in the boot and resolutely point my wheels towards Tipperary and home. Twenty years ago, I would undoubtedly have welcomed just one more adventure, but now I feel glad to be finished with the draining intoxication of new experiences and the compelling, but ultimately wearying, buzz of discovery. What I want more than anything else is what Ireland's early men of piety seemed to consciously avoid: the comforting embrace of the predictable and the familiar. As I drive out of Portmagee, the ocean is already working itself into a slate-grey turmoil, while the first rain splashes the windscreen. It is definitely time to go home.

PUBLISHED IN 2017 BY
The Collins Press
West Link Park
Doughcloyne
Wilton
T12 N5EF
Cork
Ireland

First published in 2013

A catalogue record for this book is available from the British Library

Paperback ISBN: 978-184889-315-3
PDF eBook ISBN: 978-1-84889-638-3
EPUB eBook ISBN: 978-1-84889-639-0
Kindle ISBN: 978-1-84889-640-6

Photos © the author unless otherwise credited

Design and typesetting by Fairways Design

Typeset in Avenir

Printed in Poland by Hussar Books